Welcome Aboard: More than 200 tips to make them hire you

Matias Astori

Published by Perlectus Publishing, 2018.

Copyright © 2018 by Matias Astori

All rights reserved. No part of this publication may be reproduced, distributed, or transmitted in any form or by any means—including photocopying, recording, or other electronic and mechanical methods—without the prior written permission of the publisher

Most of this work was originally published in Spanish in 2014. This work was slightly modified to be adapted to the English-speaking market. It retains more than 95% of its original version.

Original title: *Bienvenido a la Empresa: Más de 200 consejos para asegurar tu contratación*

Copyright © 2014 by Matias Astori

"Every morning in Africa, a gazelle wakes up. It knows it must run faster than the fastest lion or it will be killed. Every morning a lion wakes up. It knows it must outrun the slowest gazelle or it will starve to death.

It doesn't matter whether you are a lion or a gazelle: when the sun comes up, you'd better be running."

—Herb Caen

Introduction

If you are reading this book, I think you are trying to get hired. I also can say you may want a well-paid job, am I right? But if you are reading this book, I'm pretty sure you are now unemployed.

If you went to college and you can't land a job, I think it could be even more frustrating for you. Since we were kids, we heard the same story over and over again—go to school, get good grades and you will get a good job with a good salary when you are an adult.

The problem is that, as adults, there's a point in our lives in which we realize that's nothing but a fallacy—a lie. Our parents wanted the best for us, no doubt. But times change. And although having a degree meant the key for success in the past, today lots of people get graduate every year. That make getting a job, even for those who have a degree, even harder.

But wait a minute. There are people out there that didn't finish college but at difference than you, they have a job. And I also know people with two degrees that didn't get the job and the person who got that job had only one degree. Is it that unfair? It could be. But you should open your eyes and realize that life is not like in your childhood dreams. Real life is more like in the jungle—only the stronger ones win and survive. And by strength, I'm not talking about physical strength, but knowledge.

Some people say the only reason some people get a job while others can't, it's because of the luck. But you know what? Luck doesn't exist. Luck is only the perfect excuse for unsuccessful people. If someone is successful, it's because luck is on his side; but if I'm not successful, then luck is not on my side. You see, that's the perfect excuse. But I'll tell you a secret—only those who think like that are failed.

Some paragraphs back, I told you life is like in the jungle and only the stronger ones win and survive. And I also told you that by strength I meant knowledge. There's a Latin phrase, *scientia potentia est*, which

WELCOME ABOARD: MORE THAN 200 TIPS TO MAKE THEM HIRE YOU

means knowledge is power. It's possible you have used it in your life, or at least you have heard it. But the important here is that this sentence is a universal true.

When you have knowledge, you get more opportunities, more chances, more power. And the main reason some people can easily get a job, it's because they are applying some processes to get what they want.

Maybe they are not aware of it. But believe it or not, there are some tricks that can help anyone increase their chances to get hired.

You may think you are doing everything well. But if you're reading this book is because that's not true. And with a bit of knowledge, you can finally increase your chances to get hired.

How and why did I write this book

When I finished my university studies in graphic design, I decided to take another bachelor degree to increase my chances of success. Accustomed to working under pressure in graphic design, the new career seemed quiet easy to me.

In graphic design I got used to spending entire nights working in different projects. I also got used to work under pressure and to work on laborious projects every day with their nights. When entering an administrative career, things were different. Everything seemed very easy. I only had to read, research and write some essays. I had too much time to spare. And I came to feel like an idle person with no work to do. I found some institutes that offered diploma courses online, which would be very beneficial and comfortable for me.

Determined not to waste my time—and to further enrich my knowledge—I enrolled in various courses. Among those courses were psychology, sociology, anthropology, and introduction to the neurosciences.

All these courses complemented my fascination to understand the complex human relationships. A fascination which had begun some years ago when I began to study neurolinguistic programming. Subsequently, I spend the next five years of my life trying to understand human relationships.

While I was still a student, I often met some friends I had made in college when I was studying graphic design. They asked me about my new career, and I asked them about their lives as graduates. The vast majority of them gave me a disappointing answer—they couldn't find employment.

I asked them if they were looking for something. And they told me that the few jobs that were available were not well-paid jobs, or were in companies where they requested experienced people. That scared me a little. After all, I was still studying. And because of the extracurricular courses I was taking at that time, I didn't have time to *have experience*.

I decided to look for a part-time job to *build* the experience companies ask. I quickly found a job as a web designer. However, I had to reject it because that job was in a city that is three hours from where I lived. But the important thing was they offered the job to me. That made me feel a little more confident.

A few months later I went to look for a job in another company. This time they offered me a temporary job for only two months. They didn't need a full-time graphic designer. They only needed someone to make a professional presentation—with animations and quality graphics.

I was impressed about how quickly I had managed to get a job. But at the same time that made me think about the situation of my former classmates.

I know that being friends or not, they are my competition. I knew that if I didn't get the job, they would look for it. And I also knew that job seeking is like the reflection of the lion and the gazelle—it doesn't matter if you are the lion or the gazelle, when the sun rises, you must to run or you will die.

On one occasion I went out with a friend of mine. We started talking, and he brought up the topic of a job he was looking for. He had to send his resume and submit to an interview. He told me he tried to enter various companies without success. And he though it was not worth going to that interview. I felt a little distressed about him and suggested some recommendations. I gave him some directions and explained why he should apply them. He told me he had nothing to lose and was going to try.

One week later I receive a call from my friend to tell me he got hired as manager assistant in an advertising agency. I was glad for him. And at the same time I realized the huge difference you get when you *manipulate* the probabilities. I helped a couple of other friends and they got similar results.

Every day I used to read or listen to stories about young people who didn't find a job. So I decided to write a book with all the knowledge I had about human relations and those subjects I studied in the courses I took.

I decided to organize the information I had. But I quickly realized I wanted to write a book that will help people find a job. That would be the main topic, not human relationships.

I remembered that during my years as a graphic design student, I had worked in a newspaper project for an editorial production class. And one of my reports was precisely about how to get a job. And to make that project, I got in contact with several managers, supervisors, employers and human resources consultants from Europe, the United States, Canada, Latin America, Australia and Singapore. I told them I was doing research about recruitment and job positioning around the world. Many of them had agreed to a videoconference interview, where I got even more knowledge about job competition around the world. Not only that, but I had also obtained practical advice from people whose job it's to select human resources.

I sought those archives where I saved the information that I got in those video interviews. But more than four years had passed. I thought for a moment that I had lost that information completely. But one day, when I needed to store all my music collection to be able to format my computer, I looked for a pen drive I no longer used. Fortunately, that pen drive contained several of my graphic design projects and among them, the transcription of those interviews.

At that moment I realized I already had enough information to write a book that could help people to land a job. Not only did I have some knowledge about how the mind and human relations works, but I also recovered the information from those interviews I had with several human resources recruiters around the world.

WELCOME ABOARD: MORE THAN 200 TIPS TO MAKE THEM HIRE YOU

This book contains very useful information that will help you increase your chances of success. It's not a magic wand that just by shaking it you will get everything you want. But it's so useful to increase your chances to get hired. Or if you already have a job, to find a better paid job or with a better work environment. That is your decision.

The resume

Most of the job seekers out there believe their degrees are their best weapon when it comes to job hunting—a belief that we get for a very young age.

Parents and teachers tend to say to children their degrees will open many doors for them. And once we go to college, that belief gets deeper in our mind. Once we are in college, we are exited because we believe that at the end of the path, we will get a sort of master key.

The sad reality is vastly different. Your degree is not a sort of master key at all—it won't open any doors for you.

Yes, your degree could be useful when you are a job seeker. But bear in mind that although it can prevent someone close a door on your face, it definitely will not open any door for you. It's possible that could happen if your hold a degree from a prestigious university such as Harvard. But in the vast majority of cases, your degree is not as important as you might think.

Your degree is important—no doubt about. But definitely it's not as important as most people think.

I know I'm breaking down one of your strongest beliefs. And I'm pretty sure you might be questioning my words right now. But trust me. Even when you have thought you degree is the most important paper you have while seeking for a job, it is not—at least not nowadays.

As I said earlier, having a degree was certainly and advantage in the past. Because not everybody could go to college. And those who could were highly valued by employers. In the past a graduate was a kind of holy grail. But today, when more and more people get graduate every year, graduates do not seem to be so special anymore. There's no shortage of graduates today, so they are not special and valued anymore.

And don't forget that employers and those who work at human resources department were students too. So I'll ask you a couple of questions and I hope you are totally honest. Don't answer me—I won't get that answer anyway—answer yourself. What did you do mostly during your college time? Did you study so hard or did you take any opportunity to party? And when you were getting enrolled, were you excited about all the books you had to read? Be honest with yourself. And you will realize that college time is—for the vast majority of students—equals to party time. In fact, most of the young people see college time as the best years of their life, and in a way they are.

Bear in mind that employers know it. They know your degree is just a document that actually don't reflect your level of knowledge. It doesn't either reflect you skills and your abilities to perform any activity. And more importantly, employers know that the theory and the practice are totally different. And if you think about it for a moment, you will notice your degree doesn't tell anything about your capabilities of performing any work. In other words, the information that any employer can get by taking a look at your degree, is so ambiguous—useless at all.

That is the main reason why your degree is not as important as you think. It is, of course. But not as much as you think.

But there is another important document you need when you are seeking for a job. A document that may even be more important that you degree. A document that not only exhibit your education, but also your work experience, your skills, your competences and you capabilities—your resume.

Believe it or not, your resume is indeed more important that your degree. Or at least it is for most of the employers out there.

As I mentioned earlier, your degree only exhibit that you are graduate. But it doesn't exhibit your real knowledges, your skills nor your capabilities. A resume does. And that's why most of the people working in human resources will take a look on your resume at the beginning.

Writing a good resume sound obvious for most of us. But the shocking reality is that most of the people don't know how to write a good, impressive resume. Instead, they just write as much information as they can in order to fill the pages. They think the more information they include, the better for them—that's not true in most of the cases.

When it comes to resumes, less is more in the vast majority of cases. I'll explain why later. By now, I would like you understand what a resume really is.

In English language there are two concepts that most of the people think are synonymous, but they aren't. Resume and curriculum vitae are similar in essence. But there is a big difference you should know and understand as a first step to learn how to write a successful resume.

In essence, both of them exhibit your education and your working experience. As well as your skills, your capabilities and your competences. But the main difference is in the length.

As a curriculum vitae includes more information than a resume, it tends to be longer. And if you bear in mind that people in human resources are busy people, it's better to make things easier for them.

The words *curriculum vitae* come from the Latin *curriculum* which means course; and *vitae*, which comes from vita, the Latin word for life. In other words, curriculum vitae means course of life. Basically, a curriculum vitae is a document that exhibit our whole life. Not only our education, but also our employment history, our professional qualifications, our skills, our publications, our honors and awards, our research experience, our teaching experience, our extracurricular activities, our professional memberships and so on. That's why for some professionals such as high-qualified doctor, engineers and other high-valued professionals, it is better to elaborate a curriculum vitae instead of a resume. But of course, if your are reading this book in order to increase your chances to land a job, this is definitely not your case.

On the other hand, the word resume it's actually a loan word from the French *résumé*, which means summary. And that's exactly what a resume is. Unlike a curriculum vitae, a resume is a summary, an abstract of your life.

You no need to provide all the details of your life in a resume, but only the information that is relevant for the job you want to get.

Employers prefer resumes over curriculums. Because they are shorter and precise in the relevant information of the aspirant.

If you are a high-valued professional, then your employer will want to know as much information about your achievements. But if you are not playing in the high leagues, they definitely don't want to waste their time reading useless information about you. If that happens, your resume could go directly to the trash bin. They have other resumes to read. Why do you think your resume will be more important for them when there are more options on the pile?

Remember, your resume is only one more in the pile. And unless you prove you are special enough for them, you are nothing. Sound terrible, but it's true.

You are just another fish in a big ocean. And if you really want to improve your chances of being taken in mind, you should make things easier for employers by creating a successful resume instead of a long, boring curriculum vitae.

Paper size

As I mentioned earlier, many people think the more stuff they write in their resumes, the better. Then, going into this belief, they try to fill as much pages as they can. But as a general rule, a good resume comes in only one page.

One page is enough to write a good resume. A two pages resume could be acceptable only if you have a lot of experience. But as you'll learn later in this book, it is better to simplify your resume to make it more attractive to employers.

You may have a lot of experience. And all that experience perfectly match with the needs of the company in which you would like to work in. In that case, you can create a two-pages resume. But in the vast majority of the cases, the perfect resume comes in one page only.

Having said the perfect resume comes in only one page. I would like to speak about paper size.

When it comes to paper size, it all depends on the country in where we live. In most countries the international paper size—mainly A series—is the norm. But in some countries, specially in North America, they mainly use the North American paper size.

Why does it matter? Is it important? Well, it is. When it comes to resumes and paper size, it actually matters.

Resumes are usually printed in A4 size, the most common paper size of office stationery in most of the countries. However, in the United States, Canada and Mexico, as well as few other countries, letter size is the norm.

Letter is a little bit wider but shorter paper than A4. And maybe you no need to care about it if you live in a country where A4 is the norm. In this case, never use letter sheets to write your resume.

Why? It's too simple. While A4 is a slightly larger size than letter. If you send a resume printed in letter size, your employer will think—even if he isn't conscious about it— your resume is less important than the rest. Psychologically, smaller is less significant than bigger. And if your resume appears to be slightly smaller than the rest, the person who receives it will think your capabilities, your working experiences and your skills are inferior too.

You don't want that, right? You want any employer think you are the best option, that you are the one who is the perfect candidate to get the job. And if you want to set that mentality in employers, it will be better don't use letter size if the norm in your country is A4.

In contrast, the opposite is not true in the United States, Mexico, Canada, or in any other country where letter is the norm.

As I already stated, when it comes to paper size, bigger is better. And if you live in a country where letter size is the norm, then it's a good idea to print your resume in A4 size. Your resume will look slightly bigger. And the person who receives it will believe your resume is better than the rest—bigger is better for our brains.

This simple trick has a huge impact in the person who checks the resumes to choose the best candidates for an interview; as well as for you.

Remember, once you send your resume, your first goal is not to get hired—that's the final goal. Instead, once you send your resume, your first and main goal is to get an interview. Then, during the interview, you should convince the employer that you are the best option for that vacancy. But by now, you should be focused in one simple goal—to get the interview. And printing your resume in a slightly bigger paper size could be helpful.

I only want to warn you about something—do not exaggerate. If you live in a country where letter is the norm, try finding A4 paper. It's pretty difficult in some countries such as in Mexico. And it's certainly not widely available in the United States. But if you can find it, print your resume in that size.

However, as in North America exist a bigger paper than letter called legal, it won't be a good idea printing your resume in that paper size. A4 is bigger than letter but discreet. On the other hand, legal paper is much bigger than A4. And definitely employers will see a long but boring resume—the oposite effect.

If you live in a country where A4 is the norm, there are not too much chances for you to take advantage on this trick.

But even if you live in a country where A4 is the norm, you still can take advantage. Maybe not in length, but in weight.

Weight of the resume

The reason why bigger is better when it comes to paper size is because psychologically we tend to believe bigger is better. If we see a bigger house, we assume people who live in there are better than the rest of the people in that neighborhood. If we see a bigger car, we think that car is more expensive and because of that, better.

Bigger is better for our brains. And even when this is not the case when it comes to the length of the resume's content, it is when it comes to paper size.

As I mentioned earlier, people who live in a country where letter size is the norm, can take advantage on that by printing their resumes in an A4 paper.

Europeans and most of the people in the world can't take the bigger-the-better advantage. But they can still take the heavier-the-better advantage.

In the same way people believe a resume printed on a slightly bigger paper is better, they will also believe a heavier resume is better than the rest.

This is also a psychological perception. But if your resume is heavier than the rest, anyone who read it will believe your working experience, your skills, your education and your capabilities are better than the rest of the aspirants. After all, if your resume is heavier, it means your value is heavier too. Simple perception, but it works.

To make your resume seem heavier than the rest ones in the pile, you only have to print it on an opaline cardboard.

Most of the people print their resumes in bond paper, which is not a good idea. Bond paper is soft and get wrinkles easily. And you should not forget that your resume is your first impression in front of the employer.

Opaline cardboard, on the other hand, is whiter, more robust, and heavier than bond paper. This creates the illusion that your resume is cleaner, heavier, and more impressive—the message you want to send to employers.

If you live in a country where letter size is the norm and decide to print your resume in an opaline, A4 size sheet, you will have a double advantage. But if you live in a country where A4 is the norm and you can't take the bigger-the-better advantage, at least you can print your resume on opaline cardboard to get the heavier-the-better advantage.

There are some coated papers in the market that can add some extra heaviness to your resume. I don't recommend them at all. As their name says, those papers are coated by a compound or polymer to add weight but also gloss. And definitely you don't want a shiny resume.

Try to read any text printed on a matte surface and it will be easy to read. But if you try to read something printed on a glossy surface, you will see that's a harder task to perform.

Now imagine that the person who will read your resume will also read a lot of more resumes during the day. And you should never forget that your resume is only one more in the pile. Do you really think someone will care about reading your resume when it's printed in a shiny coated paper? It will be difficult to read because of the shine. Remember, make things easy for those who will read your resume if you want to being taken in mind.

It's so simple. Make your resume heavier, literally, by printing it on opaline cardboard. Don't print it on bond nor coated papers. The first one is fragile and light, while the second ones are shinier and are not good options to print texts on them. Opaline cardboard is your best option, for sure.

Opaline cardboard is also elegant. Maybe the most elegant paper sheet out there. And as humans, we perceive elegance as a good virtue. If you see an elegant woman and you also see a non-elegant woman; in which one of them will you trust? In the elegant one, right? This is because elegance trustworthy for us. It's simple perception. But as you will learn throughout this book, perception is a good tool we can use to improve our chances to success. Not only when we want to get a job, but in any aspect in our lives.

By printing your resume on opaline cardboard, you are adding some extra weight but also a pinch of elegance to your resume. At the end, you should take every advantage that you can to be that option that stands out from the pile.

Your resume must match with the vacancy

Many people—and I won't be surprised if you are one of them—write their resume and then send them to every company where they want to work for. They expect their resumes will match with what the company is seeking at that time.

You may believe your resume should be only one because that resume will show your education and working life. And as you only have lived one life, then you think you only need one resume.

You only have lived one life. That's true. But companies will not be impressed by your resume if it doesn't match with what they need. They have specific needs and they will hire that person that can cover all those needs.

When a company open a vacancy, they will not hire the first person who send his resume. Instead, they will read each resume—or at least many of them—to finally hire the candidate with the best resume. And for most employers, the best resume is always the one which match with the needs of the company.

Remember, companies don't open vacancies as charity. They open vacancies because they have needs. A company needs to make more money—that is its reason to exist. And companies need to hire people that can help to perform some activities that will help the company to increase its income.

If companies hire people to make more money, they will hire only those who match with what they need at that moment.

What I mean is that you must be sure your resume match with what the employer is seeking. And to do it, you should only included relevant information for the employer.

If the vacancy is for someone who is good in team work, it's not a good idea to say you were a chess champion. If the employer is seeking for someone who must work alone in an office, they probably won't hire someone who state in his resume that prefer team work.

By the way, never lie in a resume. I remember some cases in which the aspirants lied in their resumes and they didn't get hired because of that.

I still remember a particular case. At that time I was living in Mexico City. In there, companies value those employed who can speak other languages—specially English—due the commercial trades with the United States and Canada.

One day I was giving a workshop to the employees of a company. A friend of mine was working in that company as human resources manager. And he asked me a workshop about image and personal marketing for his employees.

As I finished the workshop, my friend asked me if I could wait one hour more to help him with an interview. He knows I love languages, and I can speak other languages. And he wanted I interview an aspirant who said in his resume he could speak several languages, including English and Russian.

I agreed to help my friend with the interview.

I still remember that applicant. He arrived on time, wearing an elegant suit and walking along the corridor with purpose. In other words, he looked as the perfect aspirant—confident, elegant, punctual, and apparently, with a very good education.

Once he got into the office, my friend told him that I was going to interview him.

I began with a simple interview in English. And although he could understand the most part, it was obvious that his listening skills in English were not good enough.

When he began to speak English, it was obvious for anyone that he was definitely not as fluent as he stated in his resume—definitely not bilingual at all.

Then, immediately after that small interview in English, I started to speak Russian to him. This time, even when he said in his resume he was able to speak several languages—including English and Russian—he wasn't able to understand anything in Russian. He was even unable to answer a simple greeting.

Few seconds after I began to speak basic Russian to him, he had to admit he can't speak any Russian at all. He just was trying to impress my friend in order to increase his chances to get the job. But at the end, it was a complete disaster for him.

My friend was working as human resources manager for an international company. And speaking other languages than Spanish, is really useful in that company. They usually work with people in the United States, China, Germany, Brazil, and Russia. And because they need to work overseas, they prefer hiring people who are able to speak at least English over those who only speak Spanish.

I understand that some people are desperate to get a job and they try to make up their resumes, like this dude. Perhaps he thought we weren't going to get found out. Especially because it's really difficult to find someone who speak other foreign language than English in Mexico. No one expects to find someone who speaks Russian. And maybe that's why this aspirant thought he wasn't going to get found out.

The saddest part of this story is that my friend told me that the applicant was going to get the job. Definitely, he looked as the perfect candidate for that vacancy. But as he lied in his resume, he lost any chance to work in that company. After all, if he lied about the languages, he could speak, we can't know what other lies were written in his resume.

Never lie in your resume. You could get found out and lose any chance to get hired. Don't even try it. Employers read several of resumes daily. And they have read lots of resumes during their lives. They already know all the lies out there. They know you want to impress them and they expect some people will lie about. Just be honest about what you can do, your skills, your work experience and your education. And don't forget that you should prove anything it's written in your resume once you get hired.

Lying or *make up* your resume a little bit, is one of the biggest mistakes aspirants fall into when preparing their resumes. It's very easy to fall into that temptation. Especially when we want to get hired at all costs. But it's not worth trying. You could get found out at any time. And even if you don't get found out, can you imagine the reaction of your boss when he finds out you can't do what your resume stated?

Be honest with your resume. That's one of the best advice I can provide you.

Then, what does it mean to customize your resume?

I already told you should avoid to fall in the temptation to lie or *make up* the information in your resume. But I also told you that you should customize your resume with the needs of the vacancy.

You might be wondering what it means. It's pretty ambiguous, I know. But it's simple to understand.

Have you seen there are some people out there that have a good job and make good money, even when they didn't go to college? And have you seen some other people that even when they went to college and got a degree, can't land a job?

How is that even possible? If we grew up with the mentality that those who go college and get a degree will have greater opportunities, how is it possible some non-graduates get better jobs than those who are graduates?

It seems unfair for most of us. Especially when we grew up believing that a college degree is like a master key that will open a lot of doors for us. But as I mentioned several times in this chapter, your degree is not as important as you think. What is really important is your resume.

Imagine a cartoon studio has a vacancy for a storyboard artist. There are three people interested in the same vacancy—a graphic designer, a plastic artist and a graphic artist.

The three of them could easily perform that job the cartoon studio is offering. But there's only one vacancy and only one of them can take it.

Let's put this into perspective.

The graphic designer is a 45-years old man. He has 25 years of experience. During his career, he have worked as editorial designer, as advertising consultant, as web designer and lastly, during the last five years, as photographer.

The plastic artist, at the other hand, is a 35-years old man. He has 15 years of experience. He has worked making clay figures for several animation studios. He basically has worked in the same field during his whole career. But at different companies.

Finally, we have the graphic artist. In this case, he's a 28-years old young man. He only has three years of experience and all his experience comes from the same company—a newspaper editorial. He has worked during three years as cartoonist. This is the only experience this young man have. And I forgot to tell you this guy didn't got any degree. In fact, he began to draw when he was very young and then he got some *experience* by doing some graffiti during his teenage.

So, having all this data in mind, which one do you think is the best candidate to get the vacancy? The common sense of most people will tell them the graphic designer is the one to get the job. He has the longest and widely experience. Definitely, he should get the job.

But surprisingly, the graphic designer, even when he has the *best* resume, don't get the job. Instead, is the young graphic artist the one who get it. What happened here?

Although this a fictional story, this kind of situation happen more often than you think. And most people just see this kind of scenarios and say "hey, this is unfair." "There is some kind of favoritism in there." "Something should be wrong here."

But let's analyze this particular situation.

First of all, we have to bear in mind the cartoon studio is offering a vacancy for a storyboard artist. The graphic designer may have the longest and for most people, *the best* resume. But his working experience doesn't match with what the cartoon studio needs. It's not about how long your experience is, but how useful you can be for the company.

On the other hand, the sculpture artist has worked for several animation studios. But not as a graphic artist, but as a sculpting artist. His experience is closer to what the cartoon studio is looking for. But unfortunately for him, there is someone with a more attractive resume.

Finally, the graphic artist have not too much experience and doesn't have a college degree. But he has worked as a cartoonist during the last three years. His resume perfectly matches with the cartoon studio needs.

He is the best option for the studio because a cartoonist is the closest thing to a storyboard artist. And with a little of training, he could perform that job very well.

I know this example seems too unreal for you. But trust me, is very close to reality. Not the reality in where you would like to live, but in the real world.

Of course, in the reality, you may have worked in several places. And you would like to included them to improve your chances to get hired. But don't forget you are not going to create a curriculum but a resume. And if you still don't know what the difference is, I suggest you to go some pages back.

Before you create your resume, bear in mind what the vacancy is for. Then ask yourself if your resume will match with that vacancy, with what the company is seeking at that time. And if you realize your experience won't match those needs, I will suggest you to look for more vacancies. There are others out there.

Many people want to get a job in a specific company only because they would like to work in there.But they usually forget that others will send their resumes there too and there's only a vacancy. Employers usually will hire those people that match with their needs. So it would be better for you to look for vacancies that are closer to your working experience.

If you want to work for a specific company, I'll tell you later how to create your path to get hired in that company one day. But at this time—specially if you don't have a job—it's better to start in one place than just keep trying with no success in the same company.

In other words, if you are looking a job as administrator assistant, human resources won't care about your summer job as video games seller or that job as valet parking. Those jobs, although are part of your work experience, aren't relevant for the job you want to get.

Remember, a resume is a summary—an abstract of your goals, work experience and education. So keep it clear and short. Avoid including information that isn't relevant for the job you are applying for.

Each company is different. In the same way, each vacancy, even within the same institution, will be different too. So its better to create a different version of your resume for each vacancy, matching the information you include to the needs the vacancy want to cover.

Also, you must bear in mind that each company have also its own profile. And you must get close to that profile to improve any chance you have to get hired.

Some companies focus on creativity and seek for creative workers. Other companies seek for beautiful people because they sell the idea of beauty. Some other companies focus in diversity, some others on technology, and so on.

You see? Different companies have different profiles. And they will hire people who are close to that profile. Employees are part of the image of the company. And as you will learn latter, image is basically everything. A good image sells. And employers want to sell more to get more money. It's logical that companies usually hire those people that are pretty close to their profiles because they can be sure they will keep a good image that way.

Some clothes retailers, for example, sell the idea of beauty. They want to project the idea that you will be more attractive if you use their clothes. And to send this message to their customers, they hire only people with certain characteristics to keep the image they want to show to their customers. They won't hire a fat person because that's not the image they want to be associated with.

The same applies for a company focused on creativity and fresh ideas. They will prefer a creative worker over an inflexible worker.

When you customize your resume, do it thinking on the needs and the profile of the company. If you want to get hired, you must be that element they are seeking, not just one more in the pile.

Finally, don't forget to keep your resume updated. Always include your contact data. And because of your resume will be always one more in the pile, what can you do to stand it out?

Stand out your resume

When reading a magazine or newspaper, have you seen what is that element that catch your sight?

Newspapers and magazines sell well because an important element that arouse our curiosity. Then we need to read more and get more of the information they provide. That element is an attractive headline.

Attractive headlines catch our attention because are short enough. We can read them in seconds. And they also arouse our natural curiosity.

As humans, we are curious by nature. We want to know more and more. Especially if we get only some information. If we don't get all the data, we want to get more and more. This is how curiosity works. And when we read an attractive headline, we get some information but not all the information. Then our mind asks us for more.

We like to be informed. Even if that information is not relevant to us. That's the key of success of social media celebrities. Most of them aren't artists nor athletes. They aren't even people with great capabilities to admire. They are just people like anyone else. But as you know them, if you see some news about them, you want to get more information about. They aren't relevant to you. They are normal people using a service that it's free and we all can use. But as they constantly exposed and you got some information about them, you want to know the rest of the story.

The same applies for musicians, athletes, actors, or any other famous person. They are not relevant in your life at all. But if you read a headline about them, you will want to get that information.

If you hear a piece of gossip, you'll get curious too.

And a headline is basically a piece of gossip designed to arouse your curiosity. Headlines make you want to get more information to satisfy your curiosity.

This is how powerful curiosity is. And you can use that element in your resume too. Instead of only included your contact information and your data, you may included an attractive headline to arouse the curiosity of the employer. If you do it, at least your resume will be read.

Your headline should be attractive for the employer and the company. And as you should remember, your resume should fulfill the needs and profile of the company.

Include something like: Business Administrator Specialized in International Business and Five Years of Experience. Or, Marketing Specialist with Experience in High-Impact Campaign Management.

Those kind of headline will arouse the employer curiosity. And he will take a look of your resume only to satisfy his curiosity. If your resume fulfills all the criteria they are seeking at that moment, chances to get an interview are even higher.

Do you really think all resumes are read in detail by employers? They are busy people and prefer to be more productive than only reading lots and lots of resumes. So, if you want your resume to get read, use a headline that fitful what they are looking for.

Remember being honest with your headline. Otherwise, you'll get the opposite effect.

First impressions

Another important point to keep in mind is your spelling and grammar. Your resume and cover letter—I'll talk about it later—are your first impressions. If you don't take care of your spelling, it could be harmful for you.

When you are looking for a job, you want to show yourself as a person able to cover the vacancy. Do you really think they will hire someone with bad spelling?

A good spelling will not give you a greater advantage over the rest of the applicants. But keep in mind that a bad spelling will subtract many points to your resume. On the other hand, keep your writing simple.

Remember, all job applications are read by people. And like you, they get easily bored when they read something they are not interested too much in. And if it's difficult to read, they won't read it.

Your resume and cover letter are forms of written communication. The key word here is communication. If you speak English and someone speaks to you in Japanese, you won't understand anything. The same goes for your resume and cover letter.

Choose words that anyone can understand. Your resume may be read by an administrator or a psychologist. And they may not be familiar with the technical language of your profession.

Avoid using a sophisticated vocabulary what could be boring and not *digestible* for most people. Instead, use a more familiar and intelligible vocabulary.

Remember to be brief. There will be many other resumes to read. A resume should be short, but it should not be austere. You must adapt it to the profile the company is looking for. So it should not be a problem to subtract all the information that doesn't fit the profile of the vacancy.

Every detail is important

Many people make the mistake of using eye-catching, informal fonts in their resumes. This kind of fonts, instead of providing aesthetic to the document, detract from professionalism.

The font style you should use depends on the personality you want to project.

For formal and conservative companies, or if you want to promote yourself as an elegant and formal applicant, opt for fonts such as Times, Times New Roman, Baskerville or Georgia.

If you are going to send your resume to a company with a modern, innovative and youthful personality; or if you want to promote yourself as a creative, modern, innovative, extroverted applicant, opt for fonts such as Helvetica, Calibri, Myriad Pro. And if you can't have access to any of those fonts, go with Arial.

Don't use informal fonts like Comic Sans. And never use fonts that pretend to be handwritten letters. These types of fonts subtract professionalism and hinder reading. Nobody will want to make an effort to read your resume when there are many others to read.

Align the text of your resume to the left. The New York Times notes that many human resources professionals prefer texts aligned to the left because they are easier to read.

Font size should be between 10 and 12 points. Never more than 12 points nor less than 10.

Texts should always be in black, never in another color. You may make an exception with titles and headings, which can be in some other color, preferably in navy blue.

And while it's true that creative professionals, especially those dedicated to the graphic arts, could benefit from designing a creative template for their resumes, it may not be a good idea for you.

Unlike creative professionals, whom have been trained to with concepts such as proportion, harmony, design principles and color theory, most people don't possess that knowledge. So you could take unnecessary risks when trying to create a creative resume template. Especially when it comes to readability of texts—because of the unsuitable combination of certain colors.

Of course, if you want to impress the recruiter with a creative design for your resume, you could hire a creative professional to design your template and avoid any risk by doing it yourself.

Don't abuse the bold letters. Use them only for headings and titles; or if you want to highlight something really important.

Reduce the use of italics in your resume, as well as in your cover letter. They make it harder to read any text. Use them only when necessary.

And finally, never use more than two fonts in your texts. You are writing a resume, not a tabloid newspaper nor a pop magazine.

Email addresses

One of the most common mistakes when writing a resume, is to include an email address with ironic or allusive nicknames like sexygirl910@mail.com, darknight39@email.com, muscledude34@email.com. These types of email addresses will detract you credibility before any recruiter. If you don't care about your own image, no recruiter will believe you will care about the image of the company.

Almost every single employer I interviewed told me that the use of email addresses with ironic nicknames was decisive in considering another applicant. Some of them think people those who use these types of nicknames are people who haven't yet matured and therefore, they are not reliable to work in their companies.

Get an email address with your name, such as Marco.Sanders@mail.com, Charles_Strauss@email.com, RJames@email.com. Use your email address as an opportunity to position your name, your brand.

Your name is your personal brand. And the more people remember your name, the more probabilities you'll have to be remembered. If people remember you, your chances to get hired will increase, whether for the vacancy you are applying now or any other opportunities in the future.

What to Include in your resume

Many people freak out when they are in front of a blank document. Even professional writers face this kind of fear sometimes. A blank page could be very intimidating.

But being a little afraid in front of a blank document is only one of the issues some people face when try to write their resumes—they don't know what to include in.

It's normal if you are wondering what to include in your resume. Because unfortunately, nobody has taught us how to make one. I don't know about any college program that include a class on how to create a high-impact, winner resume. And it's curious because it's something that will have a big impact in our professional lives.

However, if you are wondering what to include in your resume, I'll tell you what to include to get the best results.

First of all, you have to include your basic personal data—name, phone number, and email address.

Many people wonders if they have to include their marital status. I don't recommend it because recruiters can be influenced about it. Remember, your resume is your first contact with the recruiter. So let him focus on your experience and skills, instead on your marital status. If you get an appointment, it means they are interested on your education, your experience and your achievements. In case your marital status is important for the recruiter, he will ask you during the interview. But at least you will have an opportunity to show why you are a good option to fill the vacancy.

In some countries it's necessary to include your marital status, either by current legislation or by cultural issues. Decide if you have to include your marital status or not according to the legislation and customs of the place in where you live in.

Many people ask if it is necessary to include their picture in their resumes. The answer is absolutely not. In fact, in some countries it's forbidden by law to ask applicants include their pictures. This is because of two factors—racism and discrimination.

Despite all the laws that prohibit and condemn racism and discrimination, we can't deny they continue to be a reality in every country in the world. Whether because of skin color, ethnic origin, gender or sexual orientation, the reality is that racism and discrimination are factors that continue to prevail in today's societies.

While it's true that physically attractive people would benefit from including their picture, I don't recommend it at all. More and more companies decide to avoid receiving resumes with pictures. This is in order to avoid any possible claim for discrimination or racism. My advice would be to avoid including your picture and let human resources managers take an interest in your credentials and achievements, instead on your facial features.

However, it is also true that in some countries such as in Mexico and South Korea, many companies request applicants include their pictures in their resumes. In this case, because it is a requirement, it will be necessity to include your picture.

Apart from your contact data, be sure your resume includes the following information:

Education: What you studied and in which college. Include your masters and doctorate, if you have any. You no need to include your basic education, such as kindergarten, elementary school or high school.

Languages: Indicate what languages are you able to communicate in. If you understand several languages, make an ordered list according to the fluency level you have. Specify if you are able to speak, read and write; as well as you level of fluency.

Extracurricular courses and training: Include the workshops, conferences, and diploma courses you have taken.

Competences and skills: In what do you stand out? What makes you different from the rest? Are you a social person Do you have any creative abilities? Anything that could makes you stand out—no matter what.

Work experience: Include the work experience you have. Don't forget to be selective with your employment history to adapt it to the profile the company needs at that moment.

Labor references: Include three labor references that recruiters can contact to verity your employment history. For obvious reasons, if you only have had only one or two jobs, those references will be enough.

Regarding your work experience, be as specific as possible. Many people describe their work experience in general lines. For example, **I worked in a food company during two years.** However, you also can describe the last sentence this way: I **carried out buying and selling processes in a food company with sales of two hundred thousand dollars a year. My accounting processes helped them to reduce costs by 20%.** Both statements speak about an applicant who worked at a food company. But the second statement is more detailed as regard his previous position.

Employers want to know more than only the place of your last jobs. They want to know what your duties were.

The same goes for achievements. Many people make the mistake of writing in their resumes about their former obligations.

Emphasize your achievements instead of your obligations. That's what makes you stand out your competence. If in your previous job was in an advertising agency, you could write: **I worked as a photographer in an advertising agency, where I helped reduce the time of photography post-production.**

Although it seems simple, many people make the mistake of only placing the basic information fo their previous work, focusing on their previous obligations only and underestimating their achievements.

And as simple as this advice may seem to you at this moment, it can actually make a huge difference.

Your resume is one more in the pile. You have to make your resume stand out from the rest. This can make any employer consider you as the most viable option to cover the vacancy they are offering. And being more specific about the details of your work experience will definitely give you an advantage over the rest of the applicants.

Use action verbs

Instead of the typical, "I was in charge of," it's better use action verbs. I will give you an example. Instead of writing, **I was in charge of the customer service department.** Better write, **My role was to support the company's customers. I used to serve an average of 1200 customers a day.**

Action verbs have a greater impact that the simple "I was in charge of." As mentioned above, by being more specific in your previous roles, employers can get a better idea of your skills and your work experience.

Employers want to know your employment history—not only in general terms, but in a specific way. That helps them make better decisions. And that better decision could be you.

Social media—a double-edge sword

Currently, social media are fashionable. Social media, as its name implies, are for socializing—or at least, that should be their main function.

When you apply for a job, you need others see you as someone professional and competent. You need people think you are not only able to cover the position you are applying for but also that you are a discreet, prudent and educated person. Social media are full of indiscretions.

Keep also in mind that when you create a profile in a social network, your privacy is the first thing you lost. Your information and privacy becomes practically public domain.

You may think you have nothing to hide. But the more information is known about you, the more vulnerable you are.

Being in a social network will help you to get in contact with old friends and colleagues. Or keep you informed about the latest news from your social circle. But as the same time, it's a tool your future employer can use *to get to know you better*. And when I say to get you know you better, I mean to know you in a negative way.

Many employers use social media to get to know their future—as well as current—employees. In social media you can see how people really are—or at least that's what most people think.

Think for a moment what your future employer would think if he decides to check your social networks and sees that picture of you in where you are totally drunk. What would he thinks about you after reading those obscene comments you made? Do you think that hate—racist, intolerant, discriminatory, sexist, homophobic...—comment you made will make you look good before your future employers?

Many people have become viral because of an innocent comment that was misinterpreted. In the same way, your future employers could have a bad concept of you based solely on the information in your social profile.

The best thing you can do is to avoid placing your social profiles in your resume. People tend to see social media as real media. And maybe they are. But usually they are not given a proper use. Your phone number and your email address should appear on your resume as contact information. If they are interested in you, I suppose that information is enough to contact you.

There are some *professional* social networks in where you can create a virtual resume and you can generate a contact list. The problem with these social networks is they don't stop being social. And most people use them to socialize, instead of using them professionally.

In my interviews with employers around the world, I asked several times if it was necessary to include social profiles in the resume, since I had observed that several applicants included them. And being honest, I was curious about it myself. More than half of employers I interviewed told me that social profiles should not be included in the resume. Some of them even told me that if they were included, they would possibly be used by the human resources department to evaluate their candidates.

If you have a profile in a social network focused on networking, where you can create a virtual resume and generate a list of professional contacts, you can keep that profile. But I don't recommend you to include it in your resume either.

Although social media are not recommendable when creating a resume, it is also true they can become a great tool for networking and personal promotion. Just make sure to maintain the professionalism all the time. In other words, don't use those profiles to upload pictures of your last trip. Or even worse, pictures in where you are totally drunk.

Presentation of the resume

Print your resume on white opaline cardboard sheets. White opaline cardboard is the most elegant paper you can use to print your resume. Don't use bond paper. It gets wrinkles easily, which will cause your documents to cause a terrible first impression. In addition, there is a psychological trick hidden in this advice.

Opaline cardboard is a denser and heavier paper than bond. And when a recruiter takes your resume, it will be slightly heavier than the rest. This trick seems very simple. But once the recruiter has the perception of a heavier resume, he will also have the perception that if your resume is heavier, it is because you have a greater performance to do your job. It seems very simple, but this simple trick of perception can make a big difference in your favor.

Avoid coated papers. Coated papers are those that have a special coating that makes them matte or glossy. These types of papers impede reading of texts. Your resume should be comfortable and easy to read.

Some people prefer to deliver their resumes in loose sheets. Others prefer to staple them to prevent any sheet from getting lost along the way. If you want to *secure* your documents, use a clip instead of staples. This will depend on the person who will receive your resume or your job application. But most human resources managers who receive the requests, prefer clips over staples. The reason is simple. When they receive a set of stapled papers, they have to flip them over. That creates an uncomfortable feeling for the reader.

Many people prefer to have loose sheets and go though them one by one. And a clip makes this easier than staples.

Use a yellow folder to protect your resume and your cover letter. It will prevent your documents from being mistreated or stained. And it also will provide a more professional look to your documents.

How to prepare a resume

At this point, and after having read the previous pages, you should already know how to make a resume. However, many people have never made one. And although you have read all the above information, you might still wondering what is the structure of a resume.

The structure of the resume varies according to the person who writes it. There is no universal and unique formula for its elaboration.

However, if you don't have the slightest idea about how to prepare your resume, you can use this structure as a guide.

- **Title or heading**
- **Personal information**
  - Name
  - Age and/or date of birth
  - ID or passport number*
  - Marital status*
  - Address
  - Phone number
  - Email address
- **Education**
  - Higher education
  - Masters
  - Doctorates
- **Other courses**
- **Languages**
- **Competences and abilities**
- **Work experience**
- **Labor references**

Quote

(*) The points marked with an asterisk indicate they are not a mandatory requirement. Although many human resources managers, recruiters and employers recommend placing them, are not always necessary.

It will depend on where you live. In some places it might even be mandatory to write the information of your ID or passport. In other places it's not even a common habit to do it. The same goes for your marital status. In some places it might be mandatory, while in other places it might be optional. If it's optional, I recommend you not including it.

Consider whether if you should include that information or not according on your where you are living in; as well as the rules and customs of your country.

Summary of The resume

- Use a sheet to write your resume. Two sheets as maximum.

- Use folios in A4 or letter format.

- Adjust your resume to the profile and the needs of the vacancy.

- Don't send the same resume to several companies—customize it.

- Don't place false or exaggerated information in your resume.

- Use a striking heading.

- Take care on your spelling and grammar.

- Use a common and understandable language.

- Use fonts like Times, Times New Roman, Baskerville or Georgia if you want to apply for a vacancy in a formal company. Or use Helvetica, Calibri, Myriad Pro or Arial for creative and modern companies.

- Avoid using more than two typographical fonts.

- Never use *informal* fonts like Comic Sans or those that pretend to be handwritten letters.

- Align your texts to the left.

- The size of the fonts should be between 10 and 12 points.

- The text should always be in black—titles and headlines can be in navy blue.

- Use bold letters only for headings and titles.

- Use italic letters only if necessary.

- Use an email address with your name. Avoid email addresses with ironic or allusive names.

- Remember to include your name, phone number and email address.

- Don't include your social media profiles.

- Print your resume on white opaline cardboard sheets.

- Use a clip instead of staples.

- Protect your documents with a yellow folder.

- Include your education and your extracurricular training; your skills and your abilities; your work experience and three labor references.

- Be specific in your work experience. Emphasize your achievements over your former responsibilities.

- Use action verbs instead of the typical "I was in charge of."

Being persuasive

Persuasion is a resource used by individuals and companies to obtain the results they want to achieve. A beautiful woman can persuade a man to buy her some jewel. A candidate for the presidency can persuade a people to obtain their votes. And companies use advertising to persuade customers to buy their products.

In the same way, persuasion can be used by anyone to achieve the results they want.

See yourself as one more product on a supermarket shelf. Now imagine your competition—those who go for the same vacancy than you—as similar products but from another brand. Why should employers choose you when they have hundreds of options?

When you go for a basic product to the supermarket, a simple task becomes complicated. You have different brands to choose from, so why do you choose a particular brand? The price is a factor, of course. But in most cases people buy a product of equal or a higher price. Even when there are cheaper options.

What drives you to take a specific product? This is the same dilemma that human resources managers, recruiters and employers face when they have to hire a new employee.

When you are in the supermarket, you choose product form X brand because companies use advertising to persuade you to buy their products instead of buying a product from other brands. And as companies do, you can also use persuasion to increase your chances to get hired.

Unlike companies, who use mass advertising to promote themselves, you can't do that. You can't send several emails to the company every day. You can't call the employer every hour to tell him you are the best candidate to fill that vacancy. That wouldn't only be pathetic, but it would also be annoying for everyone. That will be enough reason to be automatically disqualified. Still, there are some ways to use persuasion to increase your chances to get hired.

Cover letter

Many people send their resumes without a cover letter. In fact, many people don't even know what a cover letter is.

The cover letter is a document used to catch the employer's attention. We can say a cover letter is a type of advertising used to persuade the employer to read your resume.

Employers and recruiters receive hundreds of requests. And it's naive to think that all requests are carefully read. Actually, employers only read the resume if it's attractive. And a cover letter is the best way to persuade recruiters to read your resume.

When recruiters and employers don't know you, your resume and your cover letter become the only references they have about you.

Would you buy a house without having seen it, or without knowing its characteristics? Of course not. And if the seller show you a picture of the house in poor conditions, would you still take the trouble to check its characteristics? Possibly neither.

In the same way, if your cover letter is not attractive, recruiters won't take the trouble to read your resume. And therefore, they will not give you an appointment with the interviewer.

The cover letter is like a radio spot or a TV ad. It must be interesting for the recruiter. Otherwise it's likely he will not even bother to finish reading it.

When you are watching TV and ads appear, it's very likely you will change the channel, unless the ad shows something you're interested in. The same happens to recruiters when they have to read several job applications. And not only that, but reading a cover letter—or a resume—turns out to be a much more boring activity than watching a simple TV ad.

In other words, the cover letter serves to awaken the interest of the person who will receive your job application. And it also serves to highlight the most relevant points of your resume.

How to make a cover letter

A cover letter should include the following information:

- Personal information—text aligned to the right.

- Name of the applicant.

- Address of the applicant.

- Postal code and city in where the applicant lives.

- Place and date.

- Data of the receiver—text aligned to the left.

- Name and position—separated by a dash—of the person to whom the letter is addressed.

- Company name.

- Company address.

- Postal code and city where the branch is settled.

- Body of the letter—text justified or aligned to the left.

- Greetings.

- Body of the letter.

- Acknowledgements.

• Sign with your name. You can also include your signature. In fact, it would be the best—text justified, or aligned to the left, or to the right.

The cover letter should be striking. It should awake the interest of the reader, otherwise he will not take the trouble to read your resume.

Your cover letter should be short—only a sheet. If the cover letter is very long, it could be immediately discarded and your resume will never be read.

The cover letter should come in the same size than your resume. If you used an A4 sheet for your resume, write your cover letter in A4 format too.

Don't combine formats. If you wrote your resume in letter size, don't write your cover letter in A4.

Use the same font you used in your resume. It's not pleasant to read texts with different fonts at the same time. Like in your resume, informal and striking fonts like Comic Sans, or those that pretend to be handwritten are forbidden. This is because to their lack of professionalism and because are difficult to read.

Don't forget your cover letter is your introduction with the company. Therefore, take care on your spelling and grammar. As in the resume, good spelling and grammar will not give you any points in favor. But misspelling and grammar mistakes could subtract you many points.

Positive persuasion

To use positive persuasion in your cover letter, use positive sentences instead of negative sentences. Instead of saying, "I never leave a task without finishing," better say, "I always finish my work." Or instead of saying, "I never argue with my coworkers," better say, "I'm very good at working as a team."

As you can see in both examples, two different sentences can send the same message. The only difference is that one example is written in a negative tone, while in the other example is written in a positive tone.

Sentences written in negative tones take our brains back to negative experiences we have lived in the past. And in most people, their brains tend to think more in a negative way—maybe because of the constant stress we experience in these days.

If you use a negative message to try to send a positive message, then the message will be negative—just the opposite effect. I like to call this effect *positive negativity*.

The best is to use positive sentences when we want to send positive messages, while avoiding the use of negative ones.

If you want to communicate that you are an efficient worker, don't say, "I am not a lazy worker." Instead, better say, "I am an active and efficient worker." This way you not only will be able to communicate in a greater efficiency, but you will also reduce any negative perception.

When talking about persuasion, we are talking about making others see the best side of us. Therefore, we must use positive persuasion every time. That is, use positive sentences instead of falling into *positive negativity*.

Cover letter examples

Below, I will leave you some examples of cover letters. These examples will help you to know the structure of a cover letter. You can use them as inspiration to make yours.

The information shown in the following examples is totally fictitious. The people's names, companies, addresses, and all the information shown in these examples, don't correspond to the reality of any person or organization.

In each example you will find some bold texts. Pay attention to those bold texts. They are good examples of written persuasion. Obviously, in your cover letter you should not use bold texts.

At the end of each example, I'll explain you how persuasion is used in the letter you've just read.

Example 1

Alexander Morkov
Greenline 320
75024 Plano, TX
February 23, 2014

Jamie Kurts-Human Resources Manager
  Jason & Edmond Corp
  Carlson Avenue 108
  75024 Plano, Tx
  Dear Miss Kurts.

Through a Employment website, I saw that you are seeking a competent person to fill a managerial position in your financial resources department. I have reviewed your requirements. And **I consider I have enough experience to fill that vacancy.**

I worked for the last five years at BIT Bank. Of which, for the last three years, I worked as financial operations manager. **My rapid rise was mainly due to my productivity and my decision-making abilities.** In the five years that I worked at BIT Bank **I also acquired other qualities, such as the developing and interpretation of financial statements; as well as the legal regimen in tax matters.** I believe that my experience could be really useful in your company, since I have the profile you are looking for, as well as the training and experience needed to cover a position as important as the one you are seeking to cover.

Would it be possible that you could give me an appointment to interview me and talk about my experience and solve all the doubts you may have? **I know you are a very busy person. So I would like that you are the one who decide the most appropriate and convenient time for the interview.**

I say goodbye to you, not without first thanking you for having taken the trouble to read my letter.

Cordially,

(Signature)
Alexander Morkov

Some sentences are in bold in the example you've just read. I will explain how persuasion was used in a more aggressive—but in a disguised—way.

The first sentence, **I consider I have enough experience to fill that vacancy,** exposes oneself as the ideal applicant in a subtle way. Saying literally "I am the ideal applicant", makes you get into the too-good-to-be-true definition or being perceived as someone arrogant. If this happens, then you are in risk of being immediately disqualified.

In the second sentence, **My rapid rise was mainly due to my productivity and my decision-making abilities,** the applicant of our example use a reinforcement to the previous sentence. Is in this sentence in which the applicant says why he is the ideal candidate. In the same way, persuasion is used to indicate to the employer the advantages that the company will have once this applicant get hired.

The third phrase, **I also acquired other qualities, such as the developing and interpretation of financial statements; as well as the legal regimen in tax matters,** creates a scenario in where the candidate avoids falling into the too-good-to-be-true definition. By mentioning something that he learned, instead of pretending to know everything, the aspirant makes himself look like someone humble and with a desire to learn whatever he needs to be more productive for the company in where he is working in. And at the same time, he mentions that he has some knowledge that could be useful in the company where he is applying for a job, in a humble and unpretentious way. In short, the aspirant is humble and useful for the company—someone who will not cause any problems within the organization.

The last phrase, **I know you are a very busy person. So I would like that you are the one who decide the most appropriate and con-**

venient time for the interview, shows respect towards the employer. Who don't like to feel important and respected? When someone asks you for a favor, how do you prefer to be asked? Like an insignificant favor or showing respect for you, showing some importance to you. I'm pretty sure you prefer people see you as someone important, am I right? Well, that's not different to the rest of the people.

People like when others see them as important people. And you future employer is not the exception. If the recruiter realizes that you see him as an important person, the chances of getting an interview or even the job, will be even greater.

Example 2

Marco Delfino
510 Mcmicken St
Winnipeg MB R3B 2V3
January 15, 2014

Andrew Schulz-Human Resources Manager
   Boreal Industries
   410 Main St
   Winnipeg MB R2V 4G7
   Dear Mr. Schulz.

After reading the notice of vacancy published in the Canadian Times (**01/02/14**) that states you are seeking a computer consultant for network support and management, I have reviewed my resume and consider that I am the right person for that position. Because I have a long career working with networks and safety solutions.

Throughout my career as a computer system engineer, **I have worked in the creation and maintenance of home networks for several companies, including SIS Systems, Compulab, Transnational Bank, Worldwide Express, and SKL Airlines.**

I am interested in the computer consultant vacancy that your company is offering because it represents a good opportunity to work with a team, something that I really enjoy, not only because it does bring me closer to other people, but also because **I consider that a well-organized work-team can increase the productivity of any company.**

If you would be so kind to give me an appointment to talk about the vacancy, as well as my academic and professional background, I would greatly appreciate it.

Without further ado, I say goodbye and wish you a happy day.
Cordially,
Marco Delfino

I bet you noticed that in the first paragraph there is a date (**01/02/14**). Every time you mention that you saw a notice of vacancy in one place, it's better to indicate the date. Why? It's simple. It's possible that there are many notices of vacancies in circulation—many of them even outdated. When you specify the date—between parentheses and after indicating where you found it out—you allow the employer to *track* that notice. So he can verity if that vacancy is still open.

Now let's analyze the first sentence., **I have worked in the creation and maintenance of home networks for several companies, including SIS Systems, Compulab, Transnational Bank, Worldwide Express, and SKL Airlines.** In this sentence it is mentioned that the aspirant have working experience in positions that are similar to the one the company seeks to cover. The applicant of our example not only mention that he has experience, but also provide some references that the recruiters can use to verify if the applicant really has experience in the aforementioned positions.

It's very common that aspirants lie about their experience when they write a resume or a cover letter. But when references are given, everything changes. At that time, the employer can call those references and confirm if the applicant was indeed working for those companies and if he actually has the experience he says he has. In this example, the applicant had too much experience, but he limited himself to mentioning only those activities that were more relevant at that moment according to the profile of the vacancy that the company expected to cover.

In the following sentence, **I am interested in the computer consultant vacancy that your company is offering because it represents a good opportunity to work with a team,** it is mentioned something that most companies are looking for today—teamwork abilities.

Teamwork abilities seem very easy to perform. But in reality, I don't know many people who are really capable of working as a team without conflicting with the others ideas.

In the last sentence, **I consider that a well-organized work-team can increase the productivity of any company,** another element that every company seeks is mentioned—increase of productivity. Productivity means more money for companies. So, by saying something like "You could increase your productivity," you can increase your chances of being taken in mind to cover the open vacancy.

When a seller wants to sells something, he will say to others only what they want to hear. That's what persuasion is about. If you tell recruiters something that they are seeking, your chances of being remembered will be even greater.

In this example, the word cordially and the applicant's name are aligned to the left. It's not a proofreading mistake. You can write your cover letter this way—it's totally valid. You could also align it to the right, although justifying it to the center of the document is more widely common. It will depend on your personal preferences.

You can also include your signature. In this example I decided to omit it, to let you see it's also possible to do it, although the ideal is to always place your signature.

Example 3

Angela Klauss
85A Southgate RD
London N1 3JS
February 10, 2014

Richard Thomson-Chief of human resources
VIP Sales
26 Barret's Grove
London N16 8AR

Dear Mr. Thomson.

Through the website findajob.com, I noticed you need a manager for your telemarketing area. I have four years of experience in telemarketing, and two years of experience in direct sales.

My academic background includes a bachelor's degree in marketing, a master's degree in business administration, and a specialty in sales and customer psychology. In addition, I am able to speak and read in English, Spanish and German.

As for my work experience, I worked for four years in the company Great Sales, where I achieved more than 2,500 sales, increasing the company's profits by 20%. In addition, during the last two years, I worked at the car agency LuxStar, where I managed to sell more than 25 luxury cars.

I consider that my academic training and my experience are enough to cover the position of manager of the telemarketing area. If you think I need something else or if something lacks to me to fill that position, feel free to make any suggestions.

I would like to get an opportunity to be interviewed by you in order to answer any questions you may have.

Thank you very much for your time.

Sincerely,
(Signature)

Angela Klauss

In the first paragraph of our example, **My academic background includes a bachelor's degree in marketing, a master's degree in business administration, and a specialty in sales and customer psychology. In addition, I am able to speak and read in English, Spanish and German,** the applicant mentions her knowledge and skills. This information is very important for employers because it allows them to know the most relevant points of your academic training without having to see your resume. In this way, employers can be persuaded to *take a look* at your resume.

In the second paragraph, **As for my work experience, I worked for four years in the company Great Sales, where I achieved more than 2,500 sales, increasing the company's profits by 20%. In addition, during the last two years, I worked at the car agency LuxStar, where I managed to sell more than 25 luxury cars,** the applicant of our example mentions, not only the job experience she has, but also the achievements she got in her previous jobs. This information should be also in your resume, but as in the previous sentence, it's a way to persuade recruiters to read your resume.

Can you imagine having to read several resumes a day? It must be too annoying and boring for anyone. For that reason, using a cover letter as a way to persuade recruiters to read your resume is one of the best strategies you can use.

Summary of Being persuasive

- Persuasion is a resource used by individuals and companies to obtain the results they want to achieve.

- Companies use persuasion to make you buy their products. In the same way, you can use persuasion to increase your chances to get hired.

- Employers receive several job applications. Use persuasion to make them read your resume.

- The best way to use persuasion to make recruiters read your resume is by a cover letter.

- The cover letter is a document used to get the employer's attention.

- We could say that a cover letter is a type of advertising used to persuade the recruiter to read your resume.

- Recruiters don't know you. So, your resume and your cover letter become the only references they have about you.

- Your cover letter should be attractive and easy to read to captivate the recruiter.

- If your cover letter is boring and doesn't catch the attention of the recruiter, it's likely that he won't take the time to read your resume.

- The cover letter serves to awaken the interest of the person who will receive your job application.

- The cover letter also serves to highlight the most relevant points of your resume.

- The cover letter must be one page length or less.

- If the cover letter is very long, it may not be read.

- Review in this chapter the data that a cover letter must include.

- The sheet of your cover letter should be the same size as the sheet of your resume.

- Use the same font used in your resume.

- Don't use striking fonts like Comic Sans nor those that pretend to be handwritten text.

- As in your resume, your good spelling will not give you points in favor, but misspelling and bad grammar could subtract many points to you.

- Use positive persuasion. That is, write your cover letter in using positive words and sentences.

- Avoid positive negativity. That is, don't use negative words or sentences to refer something positive.

- Review the examples of cover letter in this chapter and their respective explanations.

Sending your resume by email

Many companies offer the possibility of receiving resumes by email. Receiving resumes by email is an option that applicants appreciate, as it turns out to be faster and more comfortable.

Before sending your resume by email, make sure the company you are going to send it to, offers that possibility.

Sending your resume by email offers many advantages, but there are also some disadvantages on it. The main disadvantage is that your email might not reach the recipient. I'll talk about it later.

Among the advantages of sending your resume by email are:

- It's ecological, since you don't need to print out the text on paper.

- It's more comfortable.

- Yo don't need to go personally to the company. You can send it from your home.

- It's more economical. You don't have to make a trip to the company to deliver it.

In contrast, sending your resume by email comes with the following disadvantages:

- There is a possibility that your message goes to the spam inbox.

- Incompatibility of files.

- It's possible that your message goes unnoticed and gets lost among the rest of the messages in the recipient's inbox.

Despite all the disadvantages of sending your resume by email, you can still increase your chances of success by following some recommendations.

Email addresses of the company

As I mentioned earlier, some companies offer the possibility of receiving your resume by email, while others not. Because of the above, avoid sending your resume to the email address that appears on the contact section of the company's website.

You may find the email address of the human resources department of the company if you found a vacancy in any media. Otherwise, if you intend to send you resume by email, even if the company doesn't offer that option, it's possible that you may have some doubts about the email address that you should use to send it.

On most companies websites, it's common to find electronic addresses such as info@company.com or contact@company.com. These addresses are not going to human resources personnel. These types of addresses reach an information department or to the customer service department. In fact, in many cases, these email addresses don't even reach the company directly, but rather to an outsourced company which offers their service of customer service for another company. So sending your resume to that type of addresses is a waste of time.

The best you can do is to get the email address of the human resources department—something that is easier among the big firms.

There are several websites that work as directories of companies. And with a quick search online, it's possible to find several options.

This way, finding the email address of human resources department of a specific company is much easier.

As a last resort, although I don't really recommend it, you can send an email to the contact email address that appears on the company's website. Don't send your resume to that address. Simply use that address to ask for the contact email address of the human resources department. You may get an answer, but also exist the possibility of not getting a satisfactory response, or not getting any response at all. As I mentioned before, it would be a measure of last resort.

Avoiding your message reach the spam tray

Spam is that annoying email that comes to our inbox in order to offer us a product or service which, most of the time, we are not interested in. It's an unethical advertising practice.

Currently, most email providers offer a special folder to automatically send those annoying messages and prevent them from reaching our inbox.

The problem is that companies who send spam also look for ways to get their messages to their target audience, which have forced email providers to reinforce their anti-spam tactics—a practice that often affect the rest of the messages.

There are a series of mistakes that can turn your messages into spam before the email providers, which would cause your messages never reach the recipient.

These are the most common mistakes that can turn you message into spam:

Leaving the subject box blank: One of the main mistakes most people do is leaving the subject box blank.

By leaving the subject box blank there is a possibility that your message will never be read. While leaving the subject box blank, it's possible that your the recipient's email system considers it as junk mail.

30% of the junk mail arrive with the subject blank. This is a—none efficient—technique of persuasion that consist in creating a certain curiosity in the recipient. This way the recipient will be curious about the content of the message and will desire to open that mail only to know its content.

Today, more and more email providers are beginning to treat messages without subject as spam.

Using question marks or exclamation points in the subject: Avoid the use of question marks and exclamation points in the subject. More than 60% of spam contains exclamation points or question marks to create expectation in the recipient.

Leaving the body of the message blank: As with the subject box, leaving the body of the message blank could turn your message into spam before most of the email providers. It's not very frequent, but the possibility exists. In any case, it's advisable to avoid any risk.

Only uppercase letters in the subject: Great part of the spam arrives with the subject written in uppercase letters only. For this reason, most email providers begin to consider this practice as junk mail.

Promoting yourself: Avoid using phrases like "I am what your company needs," "I am your best option," "I can help you to increase your profits," or any other form of personal promotion.

Generally speaking, spam comes with similar headlines, so your message could go directly to the junk mail tray.

Best subject headline

Most people have troubles with the subject box. They just have no idea on what to write in that box.

The subject will be decisive for the recipient when deciding whether he opens that message or not.

One of the most common doubts in many applicants who wish to send their resumes by email is what they should write in the subject box.

The best is to inform the recipient that it's about a resume. The problem is that companies receive many requests every day, which is confusing for human resources department personnel. And being one more in the pile, you should make things easier for human resources.

The best is to fill the subject box with the following options: **Resume + Name + Last Name.** You can use this format for the subject box.

Suppose that Mr. Rick Cameron will send his resume by email. Using this format to send his resume, his subject box should be like this: **Resume Rick Cameron.**

This way, human resources personnel will know that the message contains the resume of someone called Rick Cameron.

A variant of this format is to exchange the order of the first and the last name—**resume + Last name (comma) + Name.** In this case, according to our example with Rick Cameron, it will be something like this: **Resume Cameron, Rick.** This way it's even more formal.

Resume + Name + Last Name (period) + Offer/Vacancy (number): Very similar to the previous format, with the only difference that the word offer—or vacancy—is added, followed by its number.

If we find a vacancy in a press release or a website, and we know the vacancy's number, it will be even easier for human resources personal to do their job.

Using this format, the subject will be like this: **Resume Rick Cameron. Offer 102939.** Or its more formal variant: **Resume Cameron, Rick. Offer 102939.**

Don't pretend to be utmost important

Some email services, as well as email software, offer the possibility to mark your messages as urgent. And it's important to realize that your resume is not important for the vast majority of companies—you're just one more in the pile.

Companies use the urgent priority function only for really important events, such as a last minute change of schedule, notices for an extraordinary meeting, or when it's required to report any change that really deserves to be treated as a top priority.

For anyone it will be annoying to find a high priority message only to discover that it was just a person who is desperate enough to promote himself within the company—a sufficient reason to consider you as a nuisance.

Don't use the urgent priority function of your email service. Your message may seem important to you, but it's not for anyone else.

Readability

When writing the body of your message, choose a san-serif font as Arial, Verdana, Helvetica or Calibri.

Usually, email services have this type of font as default. These types of fonts are more efficient for reading texts on backlit screens, such as the one in the computer. Like in your resume, avoid using striking and informal fonts, or those that pretend to be handwritten text.

The font size must be at least 12 points. A smaller font will be difficult to read, which could cause its immediate elimination. Don't forget texts are less readable on backlit screens than on paper or electronic-ink screens.

Your text should be black on a white background. Avoid using colored text and backgrounds, specially the red-blue combination—which causes eye strain.

Content of the message

You may be wondering, what should I write in the body of the message?

Many people block themselves when they start writing an email message. They have no idea how to start writing it. And for some reason, blank documents can be quiet intimidating when you star writing any text.

The best results can be obtained if you write your message as a cover letter. This way you will awaken the interest of the person who receives it.

I leave you an example to help you to understand it better.

To whom it may concern:

Through the website employmentnow.com, I found out an offer in which you are requesting a manager assistant for the sales department.

I currently have 6 years of experience in administration, and I worked the last three years in the sales department of The Car Shop company, where I raised the sales by 10% during the last three months.

I speak English and Spanish fluently. And I think that would be very useful in a company with international projection like yours.

I took the liberty of sending my cover letter and my resume by this means. I hope you can take a few minutes of your time so you can review it.

I say goodbye, not without first thanking you for having taken the trouble to read this message.

Have a good day.

In this example the message is sent to an unknown recipient, hence the use of the phrase "to whom it may concern." If you know the name of the recipient, it's better to greet him by name. Many researches suggest that by calling a person by his name can turn him into a more receptive and empathetic person.

Sign your messages

Email providers offer a tool called signature. It's an automatic message that appears at the bottom of the message. Use it to sign your messages.

Your first and your last name should be included in your signature.

Some names are very long or too difficult to pronounce. This is maybe the first cultural shock that many German and Scandinavian newcomers face when they move overseas. In this case, simplifying your name is a good move you can do in order to make your name easier to pronounce and by that, people can easily remember you.

I remember a particular case in the United States. I was working with a man called Wolfgang—a difficult name to pronounce for non-German speakers. Knowing that his name should be remembered in order to increase his chances of success, this man shortened his name from Wolfgang to Wolf. As Wolf is shorter than Wolfgang, and it's for sure easier to pronounce for English speakers, he could get remembered by everyone he met.

Don't forget that the more remembered you are, the more possibilities there are for you to get hired.

Your signature should include your first and your last name, as well as your phone number and your email address. Once again, don't use informal and unreadable fonts in your text.

The signature is very useful for both you and the recipient, as it provides your contact information to the person who receives your message. And this little detail makes a big difference when they try to contact you.

Attachments

One of the most common mistakes when sending a resume by email is to write your resume on the body of the message.

For best results, you should use the body of the message as a cover letter. Even so, you should create two text files: one for your cover letter and one for your resume—which should be sent as attachments.

Naming the attachments

Even if you don't believe it, the name of your files can play an important role in your favor or against you.

Most people don't take care on this little detail. And although they have made an effort to make their attachments, it's very likely that those files get lost during the selection process.

Human resources department receives hundreds of emails a day. And many of them contain attachments. This creates a perfect scenario in which minor files get lost.

Many other applicants apart from you will send their applications and their files too.

I'll ask you something. What happens when you move a file to a folder that have another file with the same name? Appears a message asking if you want to overwrite the file, right?

It's possible that the person who receives your message, accidentally opts to overwrite any existing file. And if your files arrived earlier, now they are lost.

To avoid any risk, and get sure your documents will reach their recipient, opt to name your files with the following names.

For your cover letter, opt to write: **Cover Letter + First name + Last name.**

Following with our example of Rick Cameron, it would look like this: **Cover Letter Rick Cameron.** Or its more format variant: **Cover Letter Cameron, Rick.**

For your resume, the format is similar: **Resume + Name + Last Name.** In our example: **Resume Rick Cameron.** Or its more formal variant: **Resume Cameron, Rick.**

File compatibility

Most people use Microsoft Word as their main word processor. But even when it could be the main word processor around the world, its files could get compatibility issues among different versions.

Although Microsoft Word is the most widely used word processor around the world, not all the people have the same version of the popular word processor. And a different version can cause compatibility issues. Not to mention that several companies prefer to opt for some alternative software in order to reduce costs.

Did you know that Word has two different types of files, incompatible each other?

Versions prior 2004 generate .doc files, while later versions generate .docx files. And even if you are aware of this and take precautions and decide to save your documents as .doc files, your file could create extra margins and spaces, which can cause a terrible impression.

To avoid any issue with compatibility, opt to save or convert your files into PDF files.

PDF files offer full compatibility among different operating systems. Nowadays, all operating systems can visualize this type of files. And it's practically impossible to find a computer that can't visualize them. For this reason we can say PDF files are basically a universal format. Not to mention that many email provider offer the possibility of viewing them without the need for any additional software.

Another advantage that PDF files offer is the fact that the document will be displayed in an identical way among different operating systems. PDF documents can't be modified, and all their elements are respected by the software that displays them. This means your document will not be altered when it's visualized.

PDF files, in addition, are usually light. Which means there should not be any problems when you try to send them by email.

The right time to send your emails

Most of the companies work from Monday to Friday, which means that all the email received during the weekends will accumulate until the following Monday. In other words, if you message arrives on the weekend, it could go unnoticed among all the messages waiting to be read.

Avoid sending your message after noon on Friday. And don't send it during Saturday or Sunday either.

Statistics shows that companies check more emails during ten in the morning and twelve midday. This means that if you want your message get read, it's better to send it from Monday to Friday, between ten in the morning and noon. This way your message is most likely to be read.

Summary of Sending your resume by email

- Some companies offer the possibility of receiving your resume by email.

- Not all the companies out there offer the possibility of receiving your resume by email.

- Don't send your resume to any of the email addresses that appear in the contact section of the company's website. These addresses appear as info@company.com, contact@company.com, or other similar addresses.

- There are several websites that work as companies directories. Use them to know the email address of the human resources department.

- Don't use exclamation points nor question marks in the subject box.

- Don't leave the subject box blank.

- Don't leave the body of the message blank.

- Don't write the subject uppercase only.

- Avoid using phrases such as "I am what your company needs," "I am your best option." "I can help you generate more income," or any other form of personal promotion.

- Don't send your message with high or urgent priority.

- Write the subject with one of the following formats: Resume + First Name + Last Name. Or Resume + First Name + Last Name (period) + Offer/Vacancy (number).

- While writing your message, be sure you are using a san-serif font.

- The font size of the message should be 12 points.

- The text of your message should be black.

- Avoid texts and backgrounds in color.

- Write your message as if you were writing a cover letter.

- Sign your emails with your first and last name. Include your phone number and email address.

- Be sure to attach your cover letter and your resume in two different files. Name those files with the following formats. For your cover letter: Cover Letter + First Name + Last Name. For your resume: Resume + First Name + Last Name.

- Send your files as PDF documents.

- Statistically, more emails are read from Monday to Friday, between ten in the morning and noon.

Personal image

Most of the time, we don't realize the incredible power that our own personal image has. When we want communicate something, more than 70% of the information we send is through non-verbal communication. This non-verbal communication includes signs, personal image, what we are wearing, our style, how we move while walking, and a long etcetera.

It's alarming to know that less than 30% of communication is though verbal communication—what we say. This means that if your image is not the most favorable, your probabilities to impress the recruiter with your presentation speech are low.

Have you ever wonder why attractive people get the best jobs and the best salaries?

Unfortunately, for some people, attractive people get the best opportunities even without saying a single word—just because they are attractive. This is a prove of how powerful the image we project is. And the good news is that we can always improve our image to turn it in our favor.

An unfavorable attitude

Unfortunately, many people are not aware about their personal image, and live under the philosophy of "I am who I am. That's how I am. Whoever loves me will accept me as I am. And I must not change to please to others." This is a non-practical and useless philosophy in the real world.

People who live by this philosophy tend to expect results that will never come. Wouldn't it be better to use a more favorable philosophy? And more importantly, is your image really good? Are you aware of the image you are projecting to others?

The three concepts of image

There are three basic concepts of image—the real image, the apparent image and the ideal image.

The real image corresponds to an image that shows the congruence between what is shown and what it really is. In other words, the real image matches faithfully to the reality.

When you look at a cheese pizza, the image you see is telling you that it's all about an edible product. And when you decide to take a bite and verify that it was indeed edible, you realize that the image and the reality match. That's the real image.

On the other hand, if you try to taste that pizza and you discover that it's just a piece of plastic, then it's no longer a real image, because there is no congruence between the image—a pizza—and the reality—it's not really a pizza. In this case, that image becomes an apparent image, because what you see, it's just in appearance.

In the apparent image there is no congruence between the image and the reality. For example, when you go to a burger shop, the pictures on the menu always show you a big, juicy burger that is visually aesthetic in up to the last detail. But if you decide to order one, at the moment when you receive it you see a completely different reality—the burger is flattened and thin, the cheese is dripping, and it's not like in the one you saw in the pictures. That's the apparent image—an image that doesn't match the reality. And when we talk about the apparent image that people are projecting, in most cases is a negative image.

Many people believe they have a good image, that they are educated, that they dress well, that they are kind, that their voices are charming... The problem is that in many cases, their image doesn't match the reality. Then, despite being a charming person, or in this case, a person able to cover the vacancy that a company is offering, other people may see them as incompetent and unpleasant, even if the reality is the opposite. And unfortunately, people base their judgments on the first impressions.

No matter how many times we try to deny it. We live in a world of appearances. We are visual beings. And certainly, appearances are more powerful than we usually think.

Just by watching you for a few seconds, not even for a minute, any employer already knows if he will give you an opportunity or not, based solely on the image you project. And unfortunately, in many cases the image people project is usually negative.

Finally, there is also the ideal image. This kind of image can be real or apparent. But the most important thing about the ideal image is that it reflects the message we want to send. And unlike the real or the apparent image, the ideal image has been deliberately constructed with the intention of being noticed and seen as something positive.

In our daily life, the projected image, whether by a person, by a trademark or by an organization, is a form of non-verbal communication. This means that like any other type of communication, it aims to send successfully a message.

Luxury brands use the ideal image to sell their overpriced products. The most exclusive hotels and restaurants also use it to make you believe they are special.

Think of a haute couture brand. The image they *build* around its brand is one of exclusive clothes for select customers. And even when their garments are not really special in terms of quality, and in many cases the most expensive garments are the least durable, customers who can pay their prices are happy when they get one piece of their clothes. In this example, the reality is that those clothes are not as special as the brand makes you think. But by constructing an ideal image around the brand, those cloths become an *object of desire*.

Now think about a luxury car, a Ferrari, for example. Think about another cheaper car—a Hyundai, for example. What is the real difference between both vehicles? Both fulfill their main function—they can take you from point A to point B. However, the ideal image that has been created around Ferrari, makes the car look special and unique, only deserved by a few; even when you can use any other car brand for transportation.

And while it's true that a Ferrari could have a better engineering, greater power and can achieve higher speeds in just seconds, unless you live in Germany, you will never take those advantages, at least legally. You just can't drive at high speeds on the roads of the country in where you are living in due the traffic and speed limits. And this is something that people who want to own a Ferrari forget or simply don't think about, because the ideal image behind Ferrari prevents them from seeing things with logic. That's how powerful the ideal image is.

The interesting part of the ideal image is that it's deliberately built. You can *manipulate* the perception that other people receive from you and thus increase, not only your chances of getting a job—or even a better one—but if you build your ideal image, it will also help you in all of your other your social relationships.

As they see you, they treat you

As I already mentioned, the perception that others perceive from you, that is, your first impression, is built in seconds—not even in a minute. The interviewer will have in his mind an image of you in just few seconds.

Do you know how long it takes the brain to make the first impression?

5 minutes? That's what you want.
90 seconds? No.
45 seconds? Neither.
15 seconds? Not even close.

The brain makes the first impression in the first two seconds. You only have two seconds before the interviewer begins making decisions and judgements about you!

In two seconds, the employer—or any other person who sees you for the first time—will begin to build judgements about how responsible you are, if you are reliable or not, how apt you are for a job, your education, your work experience, your level of responsibility, your level of competitiveness...

All these judgements are based on the perception that people have about you when they see you for the first time. And they don't necessarily have to do with reality. That is, they are based on an apparent image only.

Do you remember someone who you didn't like the first time you saw that person, even when that person didn't say a single word to you? How long did it take you to decide you didn't like that person? I'm pretty sure it was less than three seconds. In fact, it was only two seconds.

Now consider the following. That perception you generated after seeing that person, was it based on the reality?

It's likely that after getting to know that person better, you realized that he was a nice person, or at least he wasn't as unpleasant as you imagined. So why you didn't like that person the first time you saw him? The answer is simple. It was because of his apparent image and with that, the way in which you perceived him.

The same happens to you every time you meet someone. Your apparent image indicates if you are a person *worthy* of being taken in account or not.

And unless you meet someone who is too desperate to have some company, people will always judge you by your apparent image, whether real or not.

No matter how many times we want to deny it, all human beings are attracted to those people with better looks. it's an anthropological fact. This has been the case since prehistoric times, when human beings decided who to trust and who not, based solely on the physical appearance of the other individuals who wanted to join the group. And this *survival instinct* is still valid after millions of years.

When applying for employment, the exact thing happens. The people in charge of job interviews will always judge you based on your appearance. Moreover, often the most attractive people are those who get the job, and not precisely those who have the best capabilities.

Build your ideal image

It is important that you understand that your image should not be a limitation for you. Moreover, if you lean towards creating your ideal image, then your image will be one more point in your favor. You will have a greater advantage over other applicants just by changing your image.

When I was studying at college, I took a class about personal image. One day, the teacher asked us to do an essay on the movie *The Devil Wears Prada*. In the film, the protagonist is a girl with no taste for fashion. She buys her clothes in second-hand stores and thinks that people who take care about their image are superficial. She seeks employment in a publishing house that produces a fashion magazine, where all the girls working there wear with the best brands.

Throughout the film, the protagonist realizes that the image determines the treatment that people receive from others—as they see you, they treat you. So she decides to change her image, and her life takes a turn of 360 degrees. It seems fantasy, right? But is not. The film is based on a novel narrated by a girl who lived that experience in real life. And I also experienced something similar.

WELCOME ABOARD: MORE THAN 200 TIPS TO MAKE THEM HIRE YOU

Before taking a class about personal image, I didn't take care about my own image either. Like the protagonist of the film, I also considered as superficial any person who cared about their appearance.

I used to wear clothes a bigger size. I used to prefer comfort over appearance. I used to wear only sneakers, never shoes—what's more, I didn't even have a single pair. At that time I wore my hair long. And I never combed my hair. I used to wear only denim pants and t-shirts. I must confess I only had one shirt at that time, which I almost never dressed.

From the beginning of the class, the teacher warned us that she would grade us based on how we were dressed in her class. And at the end of the semester she would evaluate us through a simulated job interview, where the main aspect was going to be the image of each of us.

I began to change my image, not only because of the teacher's warning, but also because of the movie. Somehow, the movie made me reconsider my appearance.

I bought a pair of shoes, some shirts, and clothes of my size. I cut my hair and began to be more conscious about my image.

The change in my life was very similar to the experience of the protagonist of the movie. Wherever I went, people treated me differently—they treated me better.

Before my makeover, people didn't attend me very well in restaurants or in any other place I went. In fact, I had to wait to be attended most of the times. After my makeover, I began to receive a friendlier treatment wherever I went. Some people started talking with me when I was waiting for the bus. On certain occasions they even opened the door for me. I seemed that my life was beginning to be different.

At college, the same thing happened. Of course, there were some jokes at the beginning from my classmates. But a few seconds later, they made very positive comments about my new image. Not only my classmates, also my teachers noticed the new image I was projecting. And by the way, some people who didn't like me at first, started talking to me.

After that experience, I understood that the image we project is the basis of the treatment we receive. Not only when we are looking for a job, but in any aspect in our lives.

If you consider that your image is not the most appropriate and doesn't really reflect who you are, it means you are wrapped in a negative apparent image. You must be aware of it and start changing your style.

The image goes hand in hand with body language and attitude. I'll talk about it in another chapter, since you have to cover several points to generate a correct image through your body language.

Take a look at your wardrobe. Is it really favorable for your image? If not, start buying clothes that make you look good. Leave comfort aside and begin to give priority to aesthetics. Be aware that people will always judge you by your appearance.

Buy clothes of your size and opt for the elegance, at least with the clothes you will use at work. It's not on changing your way of being or thinking. Instead, look at it as a way to alter the decision of the recruiter. However, I highly recommend you to be aware of your appearance from now on in all the aspects of your life. You will notice that people treat you better. And honestly, that's a very pleasant feeling that you will want to maintain at all times.

I don't personality know you, so I can't tell you if your image is favorable or not. But I'm sure you know the answer. If not, you can ask for help from your friends and family. Just ask them being totally sincere.

The secret of elegance

The secret of elegance is the ideal size according to your body type. As simple as that.

It doesn't matter if you loved that shirt or that dress. If it's not your size or doesn't fit your body, forget it.

The fact that a garment looks good on a mannequin doesn't mean it will look good on you. Don't forget to try the clothes you want to purchase in front of the mirror. Observe how does it fits you from different angles.

Remember, if you look good, people will treat you well.

Footwear

Many people claim it's possible to know the purchasing power of a person just by looking at their shoes. Definitely, a pair of shoes say a lot about the person who wears them. And they are related to the success of them. Remember, companies look for successful people, not failures.

When you attend a job interview, make sure you wear a pair of impeccable looking shoes. Prevent them from being worn or dirty. Preferably, if they match with your attire, better in black.

I think it's not necessary to say that running shoes and sandals are prohibited in this cases.

Hair, hands and nails

In many societies, the care of hair, hands and nails is usually considered as something feminine. Fortunately, this perception is changing.

Your hair, hands and nails are part of the image you project.

If you are a man and think that the care of hair, hands and nails is an issue that concerns only the female sex and you should not even interested about, consider that most human resources managers will look at your hands as a form of evaluation.

Careful hands indicate that the carrier is a neat and careful person. It's not necessary you go for a professional manicure, just make sure your hands don't look cracked neither feel very dry and rough; since when shaking the hand of the interviewer, he could think you have dirty hands. In this case, he could think you are a person who doesn't care about his hygiene and cleanliness, which would be very unfavorable for the image you want to project before the interviewer.

If you are a woman and you like to paint and decorate your nails, make sure that the finish is discreet and your nails are not too long. For a job interview, the French manicure your best option.

Your hair is another very important point in your personal image. Your hair highlights or opaques your facial features. As with clothes, we often assume we have the right cut. And that's not always true.

Whether for fashion or for simple comfort, many times we opt for certain cuts that do not favor our facial features so much. The best is to go with a professional, someone with enough experience and knowledge to tell us the right cut—and even the right color—according to our facial features, as well as to our skin tone.

It may be somewhat expensive, but results are worth it.

Face skin and lips

When you greet the interviewer, the first thing he will watch will be your face.

Your face is the first image people notice about you. Therefore, you should pay close attention to your face. Image is not just on dressing well and having a good hairstyle. You have to take care of every aspect. And your face is definitely an essential part of the image you project.

The skin of the face can be deceptive in some people. You can be perfectly neat and clean, but if your face is greasy, you will look like a dirty and careless person.

The same goes for your lips. Cracked lips can make others think you are tired or sick.

There are people who have oily skin and their face skin shows unsightly brightnesses. And on the other hand, there are also people with dry skin. In this case, the skin of the face of these people looks taut and opaque.

As a recommendation, if you have oily skin, I suggest you acquire a dermatological cream with oil-regulator action and apply it on your face to regulate oil production. This way you will get a matte and clean appearance along the day, or at least most of the day.

You can also buy some absorbent rice papers for face cleaning, which you can discreetly carry in your purse or portfolio. They are sold in many dermatological pharmacies and department stores. And just by passing them over your face, they will absorb the oil from over your face.

Remember that warm weather and nervousness tend to worse the oily skin problem.

On the other hand, if you have dry skin, your face may look tight and cracked. If this is your case, opt for a face moisturizer.

Whether you have oily, dry or mixed skin, the best is to have a fresh, youthful, and healthy appearance.

To avoid dry lips, a lip moisturizer would be enough to keep your lips hydrated. If the problem is serious, you should use it frequently—at least a week before you interview.

If your lips looks dry and cracked, do an exfoliation by brushing your lips with a toothbrush. Brush your lips with circular movements and then apply a little of coconut oil or olive oil on them. If you don't have any of these oils on hand, a little of butter—not margarine—or petrolatum jelly will be useful to soften and keep moisture on your lips. Repeat this procedure every night before going to bed, if possible, at least for two days prior the interview.

These tips are for men and women alike. Remember, it's not about vanity, but about looking like the best option for the recruiter.

If you are a man and you consider that the care of the face skin and lips is somewhat feminine, consider that most of the recruiters I interviewed told me that many times they give or deny a vacancy based only on the physical appearance of the applicant.

Facial hair

Facial hair is totally unsightly in women for most people. Therefore, there should not be facial hair on a woman face when she wants to show her best image during a job interview.

In men, things are different. But the others opinions are different too.

Facial hair in men has been seen as a manly sign in most cultures—as something of men. But nowadays things are changing. Facial hair on a man can enhance his attractiveness, but it can also give him a dirty, careless and aged look. Everything depends on the perception and preferences, not of those men who wear beards, but of those who observe them.

There is a very thin line between male appeal and lack of hygiene. And unfortunately for those men who like to wear beards, all this falls into the category of apparent image.

Nowadays, facial hair is divided in two opinions. A part of the population thinks beards look great and are in fashion. But the other part of the population thinks that beards are something unsightly and unhygienic, specially when it's abundant and messy.

If you are a man, a short, well-contoured facial hair may increase your attractiveness. There are men who look well with facial hair and there are others who don't. But facial hair can also make you appear to be older than you actually are. And remember that there are jobs in which preference is given to younger applicants.

Many unemployed men have beards. And in many cases, beards generate an appearance of dirt and personal carelessness.

What kind of men wears long beards? The image of an attractive and manly man may come to your mind. Although it could also be the image of a junkie, a vagabond or a man who doesn't shower on the excuse that he is *protecting the planet*.

As you can see, the stereotypes are many. And although they don't correspond to reality, unfortunately the stereotypes and the apparent image are the basis of the judgements we make every day.

One study showed that applicants without facial hair had greater opportunities to obtain the job. When the employers who participated in that study were interviewed, the vast majority of them stated that applicants without facial hair looked younger and neater.

Remember, the interviewer is a person and as such, bases his judgements on the appearance of each applicant. The best is to avoid any risk.

Opt to shave the day of your interview. You won't only look better and younger, but you will also be perceived as a neat and attractive person.

Paradoxically, a beard—provided it's uniform, trimmed and neat—is synonymous with authority, power and leadership. A different study showed that human beings feel greater attraction, respect and acceptance towards those men who seem powerful and successful. And a good beard generates that perception in some men.

You may be confused by two completely opposite statements. Especially when there are two studies with very contrasting conclusions. But it's simple. If you consider that a bit of facial hair enhances your appeal, make sure you keep it neat and trimmed.

My recommendation is as follows. If you are young and lack experience, avoid facial hair. But if you are a person of greater age or have a long career, you could leave your beard—only if it really enhances your appeal. In this case, just make sure you keep it trimmed, outlined and neat.

If you have in mind to get a job as an executive, a lawyer, a university professor, or any other profession in where experience and leadership are the norm, choose to leave your beard only if it suits you. While if you are looking for a job in vacancies where there is some preference for young people, or if you don't have much experience, it's best to do without it.

One last point with respect of facial hair. There are companies that don't allow their workers to wear facial hair. It seems incredible. But if we understand employees are in some way the face of the company they work for the idea doesn't seem so far-fetched. After all, in the same way that employers base their judgements on the appearance of applicants, it's not surprising that the clients of a company will also base their judgements on the physical appearance of the company's employees.

Of course, the physical attractiveness that facial hair can give to a man will depend on the culture and level of acceptance of the people who watch you, not on your personal preferences. But as a recommendation, I guess the best thing you can do to avoid unnecessary risks is to avoid facial hair on the day of your interview.

Be aware of your personal image since today. Don't wait until the last minute to be aware of that. Trust me, once people treat you better, you won't want to come back.

This exercise will help you put things in perspective. Do two writings about your image. First write a letter to yourself, explaining if you consider whether you have a good or bad image. Explain why you think you have the image you think you have, as well as the advantages and/or disadvantages of a makeover.

Then write another letter. This time as if someone else wrote it to you. Make a criticism to yourself, either positively or negatively. If you think it's necessary, stand in front of a mirror and pretend that you are criticizing another person.

How is that person in the mirror? Do you think it's a nice person or not? Would you trust a job to that person? Why?

Do the same as in the first letter. Explain if the person you see in front of you has a good or a bad image. Then explain if you think that person should change his/her image or not and why.

When you have both letters ready, compare both writings and use them to identify what kind of changes are necessary in your image.

Some psychological studies indicate that when we have a mental talk with ourselves our mind starts to wander, and it's easy to lose track of the conversation with ourselves. But when we write, our mind is more focused on the problem. And by writing it's possible to find better solutions to a problem. In addition, we always observe defects in others, but we never stop to think about our own shortcomings. We are too cowardly to admit our mistakes and shortcomings. Instead, we prefer to criticize others as a form of self-satisfaction.

This exercise will help you to realize your mistakes and image defects. And at the same time it will help you find possible solutions to improve them.

Summary of Personal image

- More than 70% of the information we send and perceive is given through non-verbal communication.

- Attractive people get better job opportunities.

- Non-verbal communication includes, among other things, gestures, signs, personal image, dressing, style, and the way you walk.

- Less than 30% of communication is though verbal communication.

- Get rid of the philosophy of "I am who I am. This is how I am, and people should accept me." It never provides positive results.

- There are three basic concepts of image—the real image, the apparent image and the ideal image.

- The real image is one that faithfully match to reality. It can be positive or negative.

- The apparent image is one that shows something different from reality. It can be positive or negative. Although it's often negative.

- The ideal image is one that has been deliberately constructed to project a positive image, regardless of whether it's real or apparent.

- The first impression is built in just two seconds. Forget the myth that it's built in one or several minutes.

- Human beings are instinctively attracted to attractive people.

- You only have two seconds before the interviewer start making decisions and judgement about you based on your appearance.

- As they see you, they treat you. If you look good, they treat you well.

- The image goes hand in hand with body language and attitude.

- The secret of elegance is the right size according to your body type.

- Only because a garment looks good on the counter or on the mannequin, doesn't mean it will suit you. Remember to try on your clothes in front of a mirror before buying them.

- For a job interview, use black shoes. Make sure they look impeccable.

- Make sure your hands and nails look good.

- Prevent your hands from feeling rough. By shaking hands with the interviewer, he might think they are full of dirt.

- Running shoes and sandals are prohibited for a job interview.

- If you can afford it, go with a professional stylist and ask for a cut according to your face type.

- Use a lip moisturizer to keep your lips from looking dry and cracked.

- Make sure your face looks clean, fresh and radiant. If you have oily or mixed skin, you can use a moisturizing cream with matte effect and oil regulator. If you have dry skin, use a facial moisturizer.

- If your lips look very dry and cracked, exfoliate them by making circular movements with a toothbrush every night before going to bed, Don't forget to moisturize them after exfoliation.

- It's preferable to avoid facial hair on the day of your interview. However, if facial hair really enhances your attractiveness, be sure it's trimmed, outlined and neat.

Body language and attitude

Once you have understood that your appearance influences the judgement and perceptions that human resources managers may have about you just by watching you a couple of seconds, you will have understood that it's necessary to adjust your image to look more competent. That is, create your ideal image.

Physical appearance is not everything when talking about image. There are two other concepts you must understand and at the same time put into practice—body language and attitude.

Body language

Body language is the way body expresses itself. Recent research has shown that a person's brain is able to determine how another person feels just by looking at his face and body posture.

Many people suffer abuses and humiliations by others because their body language that indicates submission. Then, people abuse them, knowing that they will not defend themselves.

How do abusers know their *victims* will not defend themselves? Easy. Although they have never read anything about body language, their brains, based on the body language of their *victims*, instinctively tell them that they are not a threat to them. In the same way, anyone can know who is a threat and who is not.

This quality helped human beings to survive before societies and legal norms existed; when anyone could murder another person without any sanction. And although we are very far from those times, those instincts are still written in our DNA.

Nowadays we don't need to be as defensive as in those times, but we still do it every day. It's no longer necessary to know who is a threat or a possible collaborator, but every day we unconsciously use judgements to determinate whether a person is good for our company or not.

It's not necessary for someone to tell us a single word. Just by looking at their body posture and face expression, we already know if we like them or not, if they have social skills of if they are *losers*, if they are successful or totally failure...

Tell me if this doesn't happen to you every day. Every day we make judgements based on the image and body language of the people we observe. It's instinctive and natural for us as species. And just as the way we dress can generate an erroneous perception about us, body language could also play against us. And once again, we'll project a negative apparent image.

You can have the best wardrobe in the world and the best hairstyle according to your personality and your face. But even having all that, if your body language indicates otherwise, people will think "That person wants to be someone who is not."

Why even having the same clothes, same hairstyle and same body type, some are *cool* while others are *out*, or even *wannabe*? That's because although they have the same attire, the body language they project is different.

The attitude

Another concept related to the image is attitude. Attitude goes hand in hand with body language. Recent studies point out that although our attitude and feelings change our posture and body language, it's also possible to *readjust* our attitude just by changing our posture and body language.

You can do the following experiment.

Next time you are angry or sad, put a smile on your face for a few seconds. Little by little, your annoyance or sadness will begin to disappear.

If you are very angry, try to laugh out aloud—even if you have no reason to do so. You will realize that your anger will disappear.

If you are happy, make an angry or bored face and you will feel different too.

Do I need to describe you how an angry or bored face is? Of course not. Your brain knows exactly how to identify it and at the same time, how to imitate it.

The same studies suggest that if you want to feel more confident, you just have to walk straight, with you head held high. Or you could also stand for two minutes with your legs apart and your hands on your hips, as if you were as powerful superhero. Believe me, the change in your attitude is almost instantaneous. Both poses are what in body language we call *power poses*. And it has been discovered that by maintaining a power pose, testosterone is increased by up to 20% in both men and women, which reduces our shyness and increase our confidence and assertiveness.

William James, an American philosopher, said: "If you want a quality, act as if you already have it." This is nothing mystical or anything taken from a New Thought self-help book, or anything like that. Indeed, when we act as if we were a different person, or when we pretend to act with certain attitude, our brains release certain substances that interact within our body—substances that make our body language and posture change as well. And once the body language has changed, people around us will begin to perceive our presence differently.

This is the principle used by actors. There are actors who are loved or hated because of the roles they have played—which don't reflect their real personality. But by pretending to be like their characters, their body language, their way of being, and even their voice tone, they changed and made people generate judgments and perceptions based on the attitude of the characters in the story, but not in function of the real personality of the actors that interpret them. The brains of the spectators generate empathy or contempt based solely on the performance of the actor. And acting is nothing more than the combination of a certain body language and a simulated attitude.

Show yourself as a confident person

What do you have to know to increase your chances of success in a job interview? First of all, you have to show yourself as a confident person. Begin walking upright, with your head held high and facing the horizon. Successful people walk with their heads held high.

In most primates, including humans, being tall and big is synonymous with leadership. When people see someone walking upright, they see that person as someone who is successful, confident, and with the qualities of a leader.

On the other hand, a person who walks stooped and with his eyes pointing towards the ground, is perceived as insecure, unsuccessful, antisocial—in sort, as a failed.

Start walking upright, looking towards the horizon. You will notice that you will feel more secure and powerful in a few seconds. It's even possible that others begin to perceive you differently.

Walk a little slower and more relaxed than usual, but not too slow. That is, learn to walk without haste. We humans tend to watch to relaxed people as elegant and successful people.

When we see someone walking quickly, or even running, we usually think that person is rushed and anxious; which means that person is delayed, impatient and possibly irresponsible. Companies don't look for people with those characteristics. They look for relaxed, punctual and efficient people. The best way to pretend elegance, patience and punctuality, is by walking a little slower than usual. Just imagine how elegant, powerful people walk—those who have all the time in the world and lack worries.

The power of smile

Smiling is the form that primates, including humans, use to avoid being perceived as a threat. The smile is one of the best ways to create a good connection with another person.

Most human beings smile instinctively when someone smiles at them first. And remember that when a person smiles, no matter why he does it, his brain slowly begins to change his mood. That's the reason why people who smile frequently often have more friends.

However, it should be mentioned that the power of smile is influenced by cultural perception. In Russia, for example, they not usually seen to smile at strangers, because it's considered an act of hypocrisy.

It should also be mentioned that according to some studies, men seems more dominant, assertive and confident when they don't show emotion—something that English-speakers call *poker face*. In this case, a light smile, with a slight nod, would be better. However, researches has shown that in the case of women, it's always better to smile. It makes them look more feminine, cheerful and trustworthy.

Your handshake says more about your than you think

Get used to giving a firm handshake—neither very strong nor very loose. A firm handshake reflects assurance, confidence and leadership. On the other hand, a very strong handshake could be perceived as an attempt at imposition, and no superior likes his subordinates feel superior to him.

On the other hand, a loose handshake will make you look passive, insecure and unable to make decisions.

The handshake must fit the person we will shake hands with. In case we want to shake hands with a woman, we should give a softer handshake than a corpulent man.

A look is worth a thousand words

Get used to looking people into the eyes when they are speaking to you. It shows we trust and we are trustworthy. In most cultures, specially in Western cultures, eye contact is seen as the greatest token of sincerity and respect.

One way to get used to looking people to their eyes is to try to notice what color their eyes are.

Many people are unable to look at other people's eyes, as they are usually very insecure and shy.

If you find it difficult to look at people's eyes, focus on the space of their eyebrows or their tip of their noses. Nobody will notice the difference.

It's also important that you pause your gaze and turn it discreetly away from time to time. Don't worry too much about that. It's something natural, so it will not require any effort on your part.

Usually, we tend to look at people's eyes when we are listening and look away by moments while speaking.

What your body really says when you speak

When you introduce yourself before the interviewer, or any other person, direct your torso towards him. The same applies when they are talking to you. It doesn't matter if your eyes are focused on the person you're talking with, the direction a person's torso points is to where the person's point of interest is. So if you are looking at someone you are talking with but your torso points other way, the person you are talking with might think that you are not interested in continuing the conversation at all.

One of the biggest mistakes of the applicants when taking a sit is to sit on their side, so that one of their arms stay close to the desk, keeping their torso on its side while their head is directed towards the recruiter.

And many women tend to sit turning slightly their hips, pointing their feet to the left or right, even when their torso is aimed at the person with whom they speak. This is also a mistake to avoid.

To make sure you don't make mistakes, when you take a seat, make sure your torso is facing the interviewer and your feet are not directed towards any door.

It's not on keeping yourself strictly in front of the interviewer, but it's important that your torso is directed towards the person you are talking with. There may be a slight inclination of your torso, but make sure that *slight inclination* doesn't exceed twenty degrees.

Avoid any physical barriers

When you are talking with the interviewer, avoid any physical barrier between you and him. Avoid that your portfolio or any other object creates a barrier that stands between you both—that includes cups and glasses too. Also, avoid interlacing your hand's fingers or crossing your arms and legs.

Barriers indicate that you are not willing to listen, or that you don't agree with what they are saying. Unfortunately, people are not aware on it, but recruiters do.

Human resources staff are sometimes composed by psychologists. If this is the case, it's likely they will try to study your body language.

Barriers don't necessarily indicate that you are not willing to listen. If you are in a job interview, it means you are interested. However, nerves can make you interlace your fingers or cross your arms and legs. After all, crossing arms and legs is a natural reaction to anything that make us feel uncomfortable. Usually, we cross our arms when we are before a group of strangers, since we don't feel comfortable in a situation like that.

Most mammals walk on four legs, but we human beings began to walk upright millions of years ago. In this way, by stopping walking on all fours and starting walking upright, our vital organs are continually exposed and vulnerable. For this reason, we instinctively tend to cross our arms when we are uncomfortable or nervous. After all, crossing your arms would mean that you don't trust others and that you are not willing to cooperate with them. In the past, cooperation was vital for survival, so a non-cooperative person was—and still is—not fit to join a group.

Whatever the reason why you place a barrier, the interviewer may consider that you are not interested. So the best way to create a good impression is by avoiding creating barriers. And like all the tips in this chapter, this tip not only will it be of great help to make a good impression before any recruiter, but it will also be very useful when you want to try to socialize with new people.

Hands also speak

Hands can be used to *enrich* our words.

Most people use their hands while speaking when they are sincere. But in the case of a job interview, it's better to use them discreetly.

You can use your hands to subtly point out your resume or yourself, but it's important understand that you should not use them in a violent and invasive way. That is, not point out in an authoritarian way, nor pass them through the face of the interviewer. That will not only seems strange to him, but it could also bother him.

Physical contact

Physical contact is one of the more effective ways to create empathy between two people. When someone touches another person, the brains of both people release a neurotransmitter called oxytocin—a hormone that makes us feel loved and protected. Oxytocin is often known as the *love hormone,* because when is released by the brain, it makes us fell happy and loved by the people we are with.

Although physical contact is a way to release oxytocin between people, there is also the possibility that the other person shows rejection when gets touched. In that case, oxytocin will create the opposite effect—it will put that person on the defensive.

Some people like to pat at people's backs or touch other people's arms as a way to get attention, or simply because they like physical contact. But other people dislike physical contact, either because of cultural issues or because of prejudices about physical contact—usually sexual prejudices.

It's best to avoid risks and show respect to the interviewer, As you don't know the person who is going to interview you, the best is not pat his shoulder or back.

Normally, patting someone's back or shoulder is a sign of approval. So remember that you will not approve your interviewer, but he will give you his approval or not.

Take your hands out of your pockets

When you are talking with the interviewer, or with any other person, avoid keeping your hands in your pockets. Keeping your hands in your pockets while speaking or listening can mean indifference and bad manners, although it could be also a clear indicator that you are a very insecure person with no social skills.

Also, don't walk with your hands in your pockets. If it's a deeply rooted habit, try to eliminate it a few days prior your interview. When someone walks with their hands in their pockets, their body language communicates failure and dejection.

Practice your body language from today

It's very important that you start practicing your body language and your attitude—and keeping practice it every day. Don't wait until the day of your interview. Otherwise, you will feel uncomfortable, which will cause your body language to change to one that indicates insecurity. And most likely you will be perceived as unable to fill the position.

The attitude must be practiced and kept every day. You can start today. You will notice that you will feel like a different person.

Summary of Body language and attitude

- Show yourself to others as a confident person.

- Get used to walking upright, with your head up and looking towards the horizon.

- Walk slowly and relaxed. That is, learn to walk without haste.

- Human beings usually see relaxed people as elegant and successful people.

- Get used to giving a firm handshake. Not very strong, nor too weak.

- When introducing yourself, or talking to the interviewer, make sure your torso is directed towards that person.

- Keep eye contact—but not excessive.

- If keeping eye contact is hard for you, look people at the space between their eyebrows.

- Smile when you greet. Show yourself a a happy and social person.

- Avoid any physical barriers. Avoid your purse, portfolio or any other object gets between the interviewer and you.

- When you are in someone's presence, avoid crossing your arms, legs and fingers.

- Body language and attitude should be practiced and kept every day.

- To avoid any risk, avoid unnecessary physical contact.

- When you're talking to another person, whoever he is, don't keep your hands in your pockets.

- Don't walk with your hands in your pockets.

- Don't wait until the day of your interview to start practicing your body language, otherwise you will fill uncomfortable, which will make you be perceived as someone shy and incompetent.

What body language reveals

The study of body language has aroused great interest in recent years. Many people study it to better understand others. Others study it to improve their social skills and their communication with others. And some other people study it trying to become human lie-detectors.

Lie to Me, a television series about a group of scientists whose job is to unmask liars, popularized this branch of studies among the general population. In each of its episodes, we were shown a panorama in where the knowledge of body language was an infallible—and very easy—technique for lie detection, the reading of people's thoughts, and even as a way to influence on others.

First of all, we must not forget that *Lie to Me* is a fictional series. It was created for entertainment. It's not a documentary nor was it created as a series for educational purposes.

The plot of *Lie to Me* corresponds to reality in a small percentage. But most of it is fiction. And you should not try to put into practice what you have *learned* from the series. As you lack more information and the necessary training, you could get wrong to interpret things.

We actually could know what people think about us, influence others, and even detect lies through body language and facial expressions. But in real life, things are different.

First of all, things are not as easy as in *Lie to Me*. The reading of body language, especially facial micro-expressions, requires years of study and research. Not to mention that, as in the series, we would need a video camera to be able to review each second of recording and thus be able to find the micro-expressions, to then review the psychology of the person and thus avoid false results.

On the other hand, although such research is possible in real life, it's not something that we can resolve overnight.

In this chapter I won't talk about how to detect lies. For that, I would need to write several books that involve scientific topics. But I'll bring you closer to the meaning of body language.

Why is it important you know the meaning of body language? What does this have to do with getting a job? You may be asking yourself those questions. However, body language is something that the interviewer will keep in mind, either consciously or unconsciously.

On many cases, human resources personnel has studied psychology, possible administrative psychology. And body language, or at least its bases, is something that can be studied in administrative psychology courses. Therefore, and although the interviewer may lack more information about you, he could create judgements based on your body language.

In this chapter you will learn the meaning of body language. Thus, by knowing the meaning of your body language, you can *adjust* it to make yourself looks like someone more competent. You will also learn to recognize patterns in the interviewer and get an idea of how good you are doing.

But it's important that you don't take it serious. You will not be a lie detector, let alone a *Lie to Me* agent. You will not even learn to unmask liars in this book.

I will also talk a little bit more about attitudes and what they reveal about you. And, as I mentioned in previous chapters, it's important you start putting these tips into practice as soon as possible—not until the day of your interview.

Confidence and leadership

As I have already mentioned, companies look for self-confident people and, as a general rule, leaders get their best positions.

Don't confuse the term leader with the word boss. A boss may or not be a leader, but a leader doesn't necessarily have to be the boss.

A leader is that person who is respected and admired; whose leadership makes others follow and support him. On the other hand, a boss could have obtained that position, but if no one follows him, then he isn't a leader.

Have you seen that in some cases some employees have more influence on the rest of the staff than the bosses themselves? That happens when the boss doesn't have leadership skills—a submissive boss, for example.

Leaders are self-confident people. They are not submissive at all. In fact, a leader is not even shy. Conversely, leaders are direct, sociable and assertive.

How can you tell if someone is self-confident?

These are some of the characteristics of self-confident people:

- They have an upright posture.

- Their way of dressing is usually formal.

- They pay close attention to their personal image.

- They don't follow the fashions, since they consider that it's not something they need to do to be accepted.

- They actively participate in conversations.

- They show preference to elegance.

- While in a group, they get sure to get in the middle of the group, not outside.

- They keep eye contact while speaking or listening.

A leader has all the characteristics of self-confident people. But there are some additional features that only leaders have.

In addition to the characteristics of the self-confident people, these are some of the additional characteristics of the leaders.

- Their handshakes are firm.
- They are usually surrounded by people.
- They are usually well dressed.
- They listen to people, not just heard them.
- They don't try to monopolize conversations.
- They offer their help when they can.
- They are usually the leaders of the conversation.
- They take care of their hygiene.
- They are sociable and greet the people around them.

It's very difficult for an insecure person to become a self-confident person or even a leader. The change is possible but not instantaneous. You can try to adopt the characteristics of a leader and little by little your personality will change. But you must have realistic expectations. What you should consider is that under no circumstances should you be shown as an insecure, submissive person.

Humility and arrogance

Another characteristic of leaders is humility. Humble people often have more friends, which means their networking are wider. On the other hand, humility will make you project a good impression before the interviewer. And once you get the job, you may quickly rise to a higher position, as companies often prefer keeping humble people because of their ability to work as a team, as well as because clients tend to prefer to work with them.

Humility is not reserved for leaders. Anyone can and should practice it.

Don't confuse humility with submission. Many people believe that walking behind a person and doing everything the other person wants, at the time they want, is humility. But that's not humility, it's rather submission and to some extent, humiliation.

These are some of the characteristics of humble people:

- They like to listen.

- They don't monopolize conversations.

- If they accidentally interrupt someone, they apologize and let the other person speak first.

- They have a direct but kind attitude.

- They don't criticize others. Instead, when they talk about other people, they prefer to talk about their qualities and virtues.

- They have a positive attitude.

- They laugh at themselves.

At the other extreme we have arrogant people—those who believe that they are the center of attention and everything is about them. They are too shallow people looking to stand out from the crowd, no matter anyone else.

Companies don't sympathize with this kind of people. In fact, most people don't either. They are the opposite of humble people. If you are in this category, you should try to adjust your attitude.

These are the characteristics of arrogant people:

- They frequently look at themselves in the mirror.

- They make exaggerated gestures when they speak.

- They not only go prepared to a job interview, but also want to prove it at all costs—even if that means underestimating the capabilities of the other applicants.

- They always try to be the center of attention.

- They don't like to listen. They prefer to talk.

- They always try to monopolize conversations.

- They always interrupt others to impose their conversations.

- They are boastful.

- They are selfish and egocentric.

- As they don't like to listen to others, they get bored very easily when others speak.

The reason why companies—and most people—tend to avoid arrogant people, is because they will always try to reach the top, and don't care if they have to take advantage of others to achieve their goals. They are not good at teamwork either. In fact, they are uncomfortable working with others. They are the kind of people who think that when things go well, it's because the team is doing well because they themselves have made significant contributions to the team. But when things go wrong, they always try to blame others, wanting to remain as the only ones free of responsibility for the mistakes made by the group.

Don't show fear

Fear is an instinct we all human beings have when facing unknown events or anything that could threaten our survival, our well-being and our health. But it's also a state that betrays insecure and submissive people.

It's normal that you manifest fear during a job interview. I'm not talking about extreme fear such as a phobia, although some people may experience some type of social phobia. I speak about the fear of not getting the job, of not answering correctly during the interview, of not having all the necessary documents, in short, the list can be endless.

Uncertainty generates fear. We need to be aware of it and try to prevent our fear from becoming evident to others.

While fear can happen for the reason mentioned above, your nervousness can generate a feeling of rejection in the interviewer. Usually, those people who have something to hide, those who lie, or those who have done something wrong, are those who show the characteristic body language of fear.

The human being has evolved to suspect everything and everyone. Common sense is one of the evolutionary characteristics that have allowed the human being to achieve the survival of the species. And even nowadays, that common sense allows us to *filter* our social relations as a survival process.

As for job interviews, the fear you show can be perceived as something negative, eliminating your chances of get hired. If the interviewer doesn't feel comfortable in your presence, it's likely that you will not be considered to fill that vacancy.

The important thing is that you learn to avoid fear, or at least learn how to disguise it.

These are some of the characteristics that betray fear:

- Gulping.
- Talking very fast.
- Pushing the body back suddenly.
- Rigid posture.
- Eyes wide open.
- Getting paralyzed.
- Hands on the face.
- Licking your lips.
- Shortness of breath.
- Tremble.

While it's true that interviewers know that you may feel a lot of nerves and that you may even have some fear, the best is to avoid risks. Not only that, but by not looking like an insecure and fearful person, you will show yourself as a self-confident person. Remember that people are attracted to those people with self-confidence, and interviewers are not exception. So show yourself confident all times. And if you think it's not possible for you, at least disguise your fear.

Confusion makes you seem insecure

Another thing that make you look insecure is confusion. A confused person can also appear to be a liar. Usually, a person who lies will be confused, since when he is making up a story, he also has to make sure he doesn't say anything that could reveals him.

Confusion betrays liars. In fact, confusion is one of the indicators that a person could be lying. When someone with knowledge about lies detection want to unmask a liar, he asks confusing questions on purpose for the liar to reveal himself.

Nerves can make you feel confused, especially if you have practiced what you were going to say during the interview. By practicing what you are supposed to say during the interview, there is a small risk that things will go different. I'm not saying it's not a good idea to practice what you are going to say during the interview, but there are some people who are too obsessive, and when things are a little different from what they imagined, they get confused and paralyzed—since the imaginary scenario that they had created, is not what happens at the time of the interview.

It's also normal to get confused a bit because of nerves, but the best is to avoid any confusion.

The confusion is not only about the words we use when speaking. It can also be evidenced though body language.

These are some of the signs that people show when they experience confusion:

- Their movements are repetitive.
- They contradict themselves frequently.
- They show signs of frustration.
- They look nervous.
- They usually have verbal repetitions.
- They show signs of indecision.
- They change their position a lot.

As with fear, interviewers will be aware of your nerves and may take it into consideration at the time of your interview. But unlike fear, there is a greater possibility that your confusion can be interpreted as a chain of lies.

Avoid being embarrassed

Another factor that can decrease your chances of getting the job you want is shame. As I mentioned in other chapters, companies will always have certain preference towards extroverted people—people who can relate easily with others and who, at the same time, are able to work as a team.

Any interviewer might think that by showing yourself too embarrassed, is because you are a shy and introverted person, something unfavorable if you want to get a job in any company.

Companies will always prefer an extroverted person rather than an introvert. Because extroverted people can relate better to customers and to rest of the members of the company. And definitely, a better interaction with customers will give greater profits to the company.

Another important point to keep in mind is that shame can be seen as a sign of lies. Often, liars show signs of shame, especially when they are *adorning* the truth instead of lying, as such.

There are people who feel often shamed, but to avoid exposing yourself that way, you must know how shame is interpreted.

The following list includes the body signs of shame.

- Avoiding eye contact.
- Moving your head quickly.
- Turning around.
- Looking down.
- Talking fast.
- To blush.

- Laugh in a nervous way.
- Getting out of the office quickly.

Don't show hostility

Showing yourself as a pleasant person before the interviewer is one of the best ways to ensure a job position within the company. Earlier, I mentioned that people can feel attraction or rejection by others. And this applies to all kind of social relations, including labor relations.

Most people want to give a good impression to the interviews. That means most people will try to show themselves as nice and trusting people. However, many people, without realizing it, could manifest hostility instead of sympathy, which creates a strong feeling of rejection in the interviewer, instead of causing attraction or sympathy.

There are people who without knowing why, dislike everyone, or at least most people. They are people who try to do things well with others. They want—and try—to be nice. But people always have a bad image about them. This happens because their body language manifests hostility, regardless of whether those are their real intentions.

Do you remember what the apparent image is? It's exactly what happens with people who want to be nice but manifest hostility. What happens is that their body language is not congruent with what they want to communicate. And for that reason, the recipient of the message, in this case the interviewer, is guided by the body language of the person. And even if the interviewer has no knowledge about body language, in case you show hostility trough your body language, or generate a feeling of rejection in the interviewer, he will take his decision instinctively.

You can have the best intentions with the other person and at the same time say very nice things, but if your body language shows signs of hostility, you will be perceived as a fake and hypocritical person—in other words, as someone who can not be trusted.

There are several ways to look hostile. But when it comes to a job interview, or any other work situation, the two most common ways to show hostility are getting defensive and showing resentment.

Don't get defensive

Being defensive is an unconscious reflex we get in when we observe or experience something we don't agree with. It's a natural reaction in human beings.

As human beings, we always want to be the first and the best in everything. We don't like subordination, although as in the rest of the primate species, subordination is part of the survival of the species. We need to agree with the leaders to avoid being excluded.

The problem is that as human beings, we are proud. Pride is part of us—it's an essential part of what we are. However, in the same way you are a proud person, the interviewer could be a proud person too.

When an agreement is not reached through dialogue, we immediately put ourselves on a defensive state. It's likely that in a job interview you will not get into a discussion. But if your body language shows signs of being defensive, it's very likely that the interviewer will disqualify you. Nobody wants a troublemaker inside the company. Therefore, if your apparent image is one of a conflictive person, you will not be able to land the job.

Remember that people who observe you don't need to have any knowledge about body language. Because people respond instinctively to body language. So even if you didn't say anything to them, if you show signs of aggressiveness or defensiveness, you could be instinctively disqualified.

The interpretation of body language is a recognition system that has helped us survive. And we have developed it over millions of years. A system that we still put into practice instinctively nowadays, even if we are not aware of it. That's the reason why you can *see* when a person is going through a problem, even when he has not told you anything.

It doesn't matter if you think the interviewer will not be aware of your body language. Because even if he is not aware of it, he will instinctively pick up the message you send through your body language. For this reason is called nonverbal communication. However, if you are aware of your body language, you can take advantage of this knowledge.

These are some of the nonverbal indicators that a person shows when he gets defensive:

- Crossing arms and legs.

- Placing objects such as an arm, the portfolio or a folder between your torso and the other person.

- Hands on the hips with fingers on the back.

- Exhaling quickly.

- Speaking quickly and in high tone.

- Squeezing the lips.

- Tightening the teeth.

- Clenching your fists.

- Staring and threatening look.

Looking like you are in a defensive state will decrease your chances of getting the job. But in addition to looking like a defensive person, there's another way to appear a hostile person—expressing resentment.

Don't show resentment

Several studies have shown that when someone smiles at another person, by simple inertia, they smile them back, even when he doesn't know that person. The same happens with resentment. When you show resentment, the other person becomes defensive and it doesn't take long to get to resentment. And when someone feels resentment towards another person, it won't be possible to reach an agreement.

Showing resentment is the worst form of hostility, since it represent a possible threat to the safety of the other person. And although it's possible that it could be only the result of an apparent image, the truth is that no interviewer wants to take risks.

It's unlikely that you will show signs of resentment during a job interview. But there is a series of misperceptions called *cognitive distortions*. In simple words, a cognitive distortion is an exaggeration in the processing of perception, which is based on a series of negative and exaggerated beliefs, which come from negative experiences that have happen to us in the past and don't match to reality.

This is the reason why a beautiful woman doesn't get some men to talk to her, since they, based on past experiences of rejection with other beautiful women, will think she is also a cold, indifferent and opportunistic woman—although that is not true.

Similarly, by showing resentment—even if it's only through your body language—it's possible that the interviewer bases his judgement on his cognitive distortions and creates a bad judgment about you.

To avoid being perceived as a person who shows signs of resentment, avoid having your body language betray you.

These are some of the nonverbal signs that people with resentment show:

- Crossed arms, specially at the chest height.

- They avoid eye contact.

- In contrast to the previous point, they can show persistent and aggressive visual contact.

- Bad face.

- Showing signs of anger.

- Rigid body.

- Avoiding others.

- They grimace as a sign of dissatisfaction.

- Clenching their fists.

To get the best results during a job interview, avoid looking like a hostile person. The best thing is you show yourself as a social and pleasant person from the beginning. But don't exaggerate, otherwise you will create the opposite effect.

In addition to the signs of hostility, there's another type of attitude whose body language will make any chance of being hired be diminished. It's about sexual interest.

Avoid sexual innuendos

It's normal to feel sexual desires after puberty. Sex is a vital and pleasurable activity for human beings. Sexual needs are present in both men and women alike. Some people are very open about their sexuality, while others are too reserved about it.

Although sex is a natural activity and at the same time is something indispensable for the survival of the species, it has become a taboo in most cultures. But what do sexual desires have to do with success or failure when looking for a job?

Each year, many companies lose thousands, and even millions of dollars in sexual harassment claims between their employees and managers. The problem is not only the claims, but in many cases, sexual harassment never happened. It was only an unethical way the plaintiff used to obtain easy money.

The economic expense cased by sexual harassment claims has caused many companies to take all kinds of precautions. From placing security cameras throughout the building, eliminating all of the privacy within the company, up to be more cautious during the selection process of the workforce.

Any sexual insinuation can raise all kinds of suspicious in the company, since it puts them on alert about a possible sexual harassment lawsuit. The same applies for both men and women.

If you are a woman and the interview is done by a man and you show some kind of sexual innuendo, it's likely that they don't take any risk by hiring you. On the other hand, if you are a man and the interview is done by a woman, any hint of the sexual type could embarrass and even bother her, which will give her enough reasons to not hiring you.

These are some of the non-verbal signs that show sexual innuendo.

- Prolonged eye contact.
- Making winks.

- Leaning forward very often.
- Listening very carefully without giving feedback.
- Exaggerated smile.
- Moistening your lips.
- Insistently drawing attention of the other person.
- Smiling shyly.
- Touching the other person.
- Blinking frequently.

There are companies that don't have any kind of tolerance for sexual innuendos among their employees. So it's best to avoid any signs of sexual innuendo.

If you are a man, avoid watching with lust any woman in the office, whether it's the receptionist, the secretary or, in case of being a woman, the interviewer. No matter the rank they have within the company, avoid the temptation to observe with lust any woman, even if they don't observe you.

The best thing is to avoid any risk that can decrease any possibility of landing that job.

Are you an open or reserved person?

People who show themselves as open people, are generally perceived as friendly, sociable and trustworthy people—in short, they inspire confidence. These kinds of people tend to have a larger networking, more friends, a better relationship with their bosses and are also the ones who ascend faster and easier.

On the other hand, closed people are perceived as antisocial, unfriendly and conflictive. These types of people have fewer friends, their social relations are reduced and less satisfactory, which reduces their networking, and at the same time, they are the ones that have the fewer opportunities within the company.

During a job interview, you must show yourself as someone friendly, open and trustworthy. That will increase your chances of getting a job. On the other hand, if you show yourself as someone unfriendly and antisocial, you will be perceived as someone without goals and aspirations—two things which companies are very interested in.

Open people has the following characteristics:

- They show themselves as friendly people and show a friendly smile.
- They keep close to people they are speaking with.*
- They look straight at people they are talking with.
- When greeting, they give kisses and hugs.*
- They keep frequent eye contact—but not persistent or threatening.

Note that some points are marked with an asterisk (*). That mark indicates that those points are not universal, they are rather cultural. Consider whether they are appropriate or not depending on the country where you are seeking employment. As for kisses and hugs, it's best to avoid them, unless it's the interviewer who does it first.

Reserved people, on the other hand, usually send other types of signals.

These are the most common non-verbal signs in reserved people:

- Their jaw is tense.
- They express little emotion.
- They cover their mouths with their hands.
- Their handshake is weak.
- They make whispers.
- They constantly look down.

The best way to not seen like a reserved person by analyzing your body language and trying to change it by body language more similar to that of people with an open character. Not only will you look more social and friendly, but you will also increase your chances of success in the interview.

Summary of What body language reveals

• Your body language reveals more about you than you think.

• If your body language is not congruent with your words, people will pay more attention to your body language instinctively and unconsciously.

• Many interviewers have studied psychology and have some notions about body language.

• Companies prefer leaders.

• Show yourself as a self-confident person.

• Opt for humility instead of arrogance.

• Don't show fear.

• Don't show confusion.

• Avoid showing yourself embarrassed.

• Don't show hostility.

• Don't get defensive.

• Don't show resentment.

• Avoid any kind of sexual innuendo.

• Show yourself as an open person.

WELCOME ABOARD: MORE THAN 200 TIPS TO MAKE THEM HIRE YOU 119

• Review the lists of signs and characteristics of the attitudes shown in this chapter.

• Don't exaggerate any attitude. When you try to adapt your attitude, try to look as natural as possible.

What interviewer's body language says

In this chapter I'll explain you the meaning of the more common body language that interviewers often show during a job interview.

Before you get excited thinking you will be an expert on reading the body language and recognizing lies, I want to make it very clear that the clues I will mention are not for you to try to guess the interviewer's decision.

Before talking about body language that the interviewer could show, I want to make some points very clear.

First of all, the reading of body language can be more confusing than you think. There are several factors to have in mind, such as cultural factors, the moment, the situation and the weather.

For example, when a person rubs his hands, his body language would indicate that that person is impatient. But if that person were in a cold place, then that argument is no longer valid.

Now imagine a person who is sitting. He is shaking his legs and is sweating. His body language would indicate he is nervous. And if he is being interviewed by the police, you might assume he is nervous because he was discovered doing something illegal. But imagine the police stopped him by mistake and they are incriminating him for something he didn't do. It's normal to be nervous due to uncertainty, and not because he has committed a crime.

As you can see, the interpretation of body language is not just about knowing what each gesture means. You also must consider a series of factors that include, among other things, the psychology of the person. Therefore, don't pretend to be an expert in body language, or you could make a chain of mistakes.

The clues I'm going to mention are not for you to be able to reveal lies. Use them to know how well or poorly you are doing during your interview. Don't focus on the interviewer's body language either.

Remember that you are the one who is interviewed, not backwards. And never forget that your main objective is to get the job.

I will tell you what are the most common nonverbal signs, as well as their theoretical interpretations.

These are the most common nonverbal signs that interviewers unconsciously do during an interview:

Open and visible palms: When the palms of the hand are open and in sight, it's a sign of sincerity. Don't only expect to see that during your interview, you could also keep your hands in sight to improve your image before the interviewer.

Intertwining fingers: When someone intertwines his fingers, it's a sign of authority. This is a very common gesture among interviewers, since they know they have the control of the situation.

Rubbing hands: This is one of the signs that reveal impatience. If you see this sign in the interviewer, he may want to end the interview as soon as possible.

Crossing legs and swing feet: This is a sign of boredom.

Stroking the jaw: If someone strokes his jaw, it means he is making a decision. It's possible that he is analyzing what you are saying.

Looking down: This can mean two things. The interviewer may not believe what you are saying, but it may also mean disinterest. Either way, it's a negative indicator. Even so, avoid being prey to despair. The interviewer is probably watching your resume, or he could also be evaluating some aspect of your image, such as your hands, your portfolio or your shoes.

Crossed arms: It's a clear indicator of lack of willingness to listen you. It's very likely that the interviewer is not interested in listening your presentation. To avoid this situation from the beginning, give a firm handshake or give your resume in his hands; or if you think it's right at that moment, ask him a question.

Hands in form of a warhead: This sign means mental evaluation. The interviewer may be evaluating a possible decision. It's a good time to let him think.

Eye contact: If the interviewer is keeping eye contact, it means that he is listening carefully.

Slowly moving the head from side to side without taking his eyes off from you: Negative evaluation. It's possible he doesn't believe what you are saying, or he doesn't agree with what you say.

These are just some of the many nonverbal indicator that interviewers could express. With these clues you can try to verify how well you are doing it during your interview. It's not on trying to know if they are lying to you or whether they will give you the job or not. Remember the position you are in—they are evaluating you. You are not the person who is evaluating someone else.

Being too focused on reading the interviewer's body language can interfere with the way you perform in the interview. Also, don't try to stare at the interviewer to observe his body language. Otherwise, you could be perceived as a hostile person.

If you see any of the clues that indicates any negative evaluation, don't be disappointed. Instead of feeling like a failure, try to *adjust* the attitude of the interviewer. For example, you can try to change the subject a bit, in a subtle and discrete way, of course. Never allow an awkward silence to occur.

As I warned you at the beginning of this chapter, these clues don't make you a body language *reader,* nor do you become an expert. Use them only as a reference and don't allow yourself them diverted you from your main goal—get the job.

Summary of What interviewer's body language says

- Review the nonverbal indicators that are shown in this chapter.

- The clues mentioned in this chapter are not to detect lies nor to know if they will give you the job.

- The nonverbal indicators shown in this chapter are only to know if you are doing it well during your interview.

- Don't forget what your main goal is—get the job.

- Don't focus on the interviewer to observe his body language, otherwise you could be perceived as a hostile person.

- If you observe any negative evaluation, simply improvise to *adjust* the interviewer's evaluation.

- Remember, they are evaluating you. Therefore, you are not evaluating the interviewer.

Building up the experience

Most companies seek for employees who have some level of work experience. This allows them to be a little more confident about their future job performance within the company.

Unfortunately, you may not have that experience companies seek. And usually, work experience is a requirement rather a recommendation.

How will you get your first job if they ask you for experience wherever you go?

Many people work and study at same time. That is already an advantage for them. However, many others only study.

But what can you do when you already got your degree and have no work experience? Are you condemned to seek employment without getting a favorable response? Not precisely.

Many people perform internships while they are studying. And although it's often a practice without any remuneration and not a job as such, it can also be used to demonstrate some work experience.

Professional practices are compulsory in some universities, depending on the career or the country in where you are studying.

If you are still studying, I recommend you to take some professional practices, regardless of whether they are compulsory or not. They will so usefully when you apply for your first job. I even know some people who were hired in the company where they lent their professional practices due to their performance.

If you are not in college anymore, you still have two options—apply for non-paid internships in a company or get a job in a position other that what you studied. It's all about generating experience.

If you choose the second option, keep in mind that you should last in that job at least one year, since that is the time in which companies consider you were an efficient worker.

WELCOME ABOARD: MORE THAN 200 TIPS TO MAKE THEM HIRE YOU

If you really want to change job as soon as possible, or if you opted for professional internships, the minimal time you should last in a job to be consider as someone responsible and productive is six months. If you quit in less that six months, future employers could assume that you are not interested in your work well-being, much less in the interest of the company. Or maybe they can think you are too irresponsible and not focused on your priorities.

Don't be disappointed. Remember that having a degree don't guarantee any employment. In fact, illogical as it may seem for some people, many graduates believe that having a college degree will guarantee them a management position as their fist job. Unfortunately, in the real world things are not like that.

I leave you a list of possible *first jobs* that you could consider to build that experience companies request. I recommend you choose those ones that most closely adhere to your profession.

- Sales agent.
- Telemarketing salesman.
- Seller of insurance policies.
- Staff in a department store.
- Claims advisor—car insurance agent.
- Makeup consultant.
- Travel agent.
- Assistant in a real-estate agency.
- Accounting assistant.
- Assistant in a legal office.
- Bank cashier.
- Staff of a cinema.
- Low-level administrative staff.
- Personal assistant.
- Tour guide.
- Tourism promoter.

- Nightclub staff.
- Kitchen assistant.
- Hotel receptionist.
- Restaurant receptionist.
- Fast food chain staff.
- Secretary.

After reading the previous list, you may be incredulous and suspicious about that. It's very likely that you think you didn't study for several years to have that kind of jobs and certainly, it's likely those jobs have nothing to do with your profession. But I'll tell you a secret. Companies are not interested in you previous jobs. What they are really interested in is in all of the achievements you got in those previous jobs.

If you worked in a fast food chain and thanks to your collaboration sales rose 25% during the period you worked there, it's something that recruiters are interested in. If you were a sales agent and you managed to outdo your colleagues, that is what is relevant to the company you want to belong to.

In the chapter in where I spoke about the resume, I emphasize exposing your achievements over your responsibilities. Companies are interested in your achievements more than about your previous job. It doesn't matter if you have had a hundred jobs before, if you didn't get any significant achievement in your previous jobs, having a long work experience won't help you so much.

Be creative in your job. If you work in a cinema and they don't sell enough tickets during a specific day on the week, talk with your manager and make him a proposal to help them to increase sales. If you work in a clothing store, make a proposal to your manager about some type of promotion to be able to sell the seasonal balances.

What I want you to understand is that companies are interested in your achievements, not in your previous jobs. Do you understand the reason for the previous list now? Not only it's a job to cover a work requirement. It's about having the opportunity to create significant achievements that will impress your future employers.

Know the company

In several chapters, I have mentioned the importance of adjusting your resume to the profile of the company. To adjust your resume to the profile of the company, you must first know a bit about it.

When you want to know the profile of the company, it's best to make a little research about it.

Nowadays, getting information about a company, and even about a person, is easier than ever. Information is available literally a click away. The internet has made information easy to find.

Companies usually have a website. And in most of those sites it's possible to find a link to a section like *Who We Are, About Us, Our Company, Our History,* or other similar links.

In each of these links it's possible to find not only general information about the company, but also some other important information such as its mission, vision, institutional values, philosophy, and other general information. All that information is so valuable for you. It may seem insignificant, but knowing that information, will give you an advantage.

Why is it important to know the institutional values of the company? Why should I know the company's philosophy? Why should I know the mission and the vision of that company?

When you want to please someone, you try to know a little about that person. You try to know his likes and dislikes in order to *adjust* a bit your way of being to look like a nicer person. The same goes for companies. The only difference is that, unlike most people, the information of a company is usually available online.

In several chapters I have talked about the importance of adjusting your resume to the profile of the company. And when you know the company, adjusting your resume to the profile of the company is even easier.

When I was interviewing employers, human resources managers and recruiters in order to obtain more information about the job seeking—something which was later essential to write this book—I asked some questions about the importance of knowing the company. Many of them gave me answers that I didn't expect to receive.

For example, an employer of a company based in London told me that he has a question that always bothered applicants and allow him to remove them from their comfort zone. This strategy is very useful to him because that way he can know applicants better.

"What is that question and why you frequently ask it?" I asked.

"When an applicant come to an interview with me, he has usually practiced a very convincing speech. He shows me his degrees and his *incredible* resume. And then, he talks to me about his work experience. They are very confident when they enter my office because they actually have already practiced their answers. They make a list of possible questions that I will ask them and in advance and practiced their answers."

At that moment I understood why he was asking that question he was talking about. In fact, many aspirants usually practice their answers. It's a way to prepare mentally yourself to feel more confident during the interview. There is even a chapter in this book in where I will talk about it.

While I was talking with this person, my curiosity about that question made me get impatient. I really wanted to know what that question was that I had never heard of before.

"I understand why you ask that question," I said. "But I would like to know what is that question?"

"Actually, there may be several questions."

"Alright. I don't want to be insistent. But I'm very curious about. What are those questions you are talking about?"

"I can ask if they know who was the founder of the company, if they have an idea about who is the current executive director, in what year was the company founded, or I can simply ask if they know something about the story of the company."

I didn't expect to receive that answer. Honestly, I had never though about something like that before. Definitely, if someone had asked me those questions when I was an applicant, I would not know what to answer. And to be honest, I think it should be very embarrassing to say "I don't know" during a job interview.

When I finished the video interview with that employer, I though maybe he was too eccentric and perhaps that was the reason for his unique questions. But a couple more video interviews gave me another perspective.

The next morning, after having interviewed three recruiters the previous day, I received an email from a woman from Montreal. She was the director of one of the most requested human resources consultancies in Quebec. She had agreed to give me an interview via Skype, though text messages. Apparently, she was able to read, write and speak English, but she was not very good when it came to listening and, in her own words, she was unable to get rid of her strong French accent, so she preferred to be interviewed trough text messages.

At twelve o'clock noon, Quebec time, I connected to Skype to be able to interview her. Several questions later, I decided to talk to her about the interview I had had the previous day with that Londoner employer. Her answer didn't surprise me so much. Although, being honest, I expected her to share the same point of view I had.

"That's more common than you think," she said. "Many employers ask abstract questions about the company, its founders, its current executive director, or they can simply ask applicants how their relationships with friends and family are.

"Really?"

"Yes. That way employers can get applicants out of their comfort zone. You see, when a person goes in search of a job, it's common that they practice their answers and therefore, they fell more confident and act in a way that is not natural in them. But when they hear a question that they had not considered, for example, about the founder of the company, they immediately get out from their comfort zone and begin to reveal their true personality.

Her answer was very similar to that of the employer in London. Someone had told me something at some point on the planet and on the other side of the world, someone had confirmed it to me.

The same day I called the director of human resources of a food company in Chile. He confirmed to me, once again, that several recruiters use that technique.

Three people from different countries had given me a similar version. That made me consider it wasn't something cultural, much less a single person preference. In addition, both in Chile and Canada, I had been told that several recruiters ask similar questions during the interview.

In short, the advice is simple—know the company. You don't need to know everything about the company. But it would be helpful to take some time to make a small research on its mission, vision, institutional values and business philosophy.

These data will allow you to know the personality of the company. And with that information you can adjust your resume to the profile of it. It would also be a good idea to learn more about the company, such as its history, the date of its foundation, the name of the founder, and the current executive director. All that information could avoid you any hard to swallow situation.

If during your interview they ask you something like the year of the company foundation and you answer appropriately, not only will you be more confident during the rest of the interview, but also the recruiter will see you as someone who really want to work in that company and therefore, your intentions to get hired go beyond your financial needs.

Although, being honest, it's likely the money is your only motivation.

Summary of Know the company

• To adjust your resume to the profile of the company, first you must know it.

• The website of most companies usually offers general information that could be useful for you. Look for links like *Who We Are, About Us,* or similar links.

• Remember to review the mission, vision, institutional values and the philosophy of the company.

• It's advisable to investigate a little about the history of the company, as well as the year of its founding, the name of the founder and the current executive director. It's unlikely they will ask you this kind of information during the interview, but even so, it's still probably.

How to dress to get hired

We already have talked about image, and how it affects the way others perceive you. You already know the three concepts of image. You also can now differentiate the real image, the apparent image and the ideal image. If you still can't distinguish between the three types of image, I recommend you go back and read the chapter that talks about personal image.

Remember, the image you project influences the employer's decision by more than 60%. In fact, a good resume can get totally overshadowed by the bad image of the applicant. Employers—and everyone who see you—will judge you based on how you look. Therefore, you should start paying attention to your personal image.

You should already be able to know if your image is favorable to you or not. If you have realized that your image is not the most favorable to you, you may be wondering, what king of clothes should I wear to get a better image. And more importantly, what do I wear to get hired?

The answer to the last question is as diverse as the professions themselves. Of course, a doctor will not dress like an accountant. And an accountant will not dress in the same way a chef would.

It would be very difficult to tell each applicant how to dress appropriately according to their profession. To talk about it, I would need to write a whole book specialized in that subject. But the advice I will mention here can be useful to anyone—no matter the profession they perform.

In this chapter, I'll explain some points to keep in mind when considering your clothes, regardless of your profession. I also will explain the most common mistakes when dressing, both in men and women, as well as some tips to improve your appearance.

WELCOME ABOARD: MORE THAN 200 TIPS TO MAKE THEM HIRE YOU

I decided to start by talking about the most common mistakes in clothing so you can begin to evaluate how you dress—or have thought about dressing—in your interviews.

I think your time is very value to waste. That's why I will talk about the mistakes and clothing tips for men and women separately. This way, you can read only those tips referring to your gender while avoid those that will not be useful for you at all.

Most common mistakes in women

Women are, in most cases, fanatical about shopping. They love buying clothes, jewelry, shoes and accessories. For that reason, fashion and footwear designers seem to be more focused on the female market. The variety of footwear and clothing for women far exceeds the male offer.

You can find a wide variety of clothes, shoes, jewelry and bags in stores. Some of those articles are very discreet, while in other cases, to say that some of those articles fall into the definition of eccentricity, is to fall short.

Tastes in dressing vary from woman to woman. Some women get right and others, let's accept it, they are far from elegance.

Regardless of your fashion sense and the opinion of your friends and family, you may make several dress mistakes when going to a job interview.

These are the most common dress mistakes committed by women:

Too short skirts: When we say image is important to get a job, many women think, in a wrong way, that they have to look sexy to convince the employer, who is usually a man. This is one of the main mistakes of women.

Remember that you are being evaluated and every aspect counts. Do you remember what we talked about sexual innuendos, and how they affect your chances of getting the job you're looking for? Well, short skirts could fit the definition of *sexual innuendo*. It's about seeing yourself as a discreet, elegant and competent person. If you plan to wear a short skirt to your job interview, just remember those cliches about sensual women. In simple words, short skirts are not recommended at all.

Too big earrings and jewelry: Earrings and jewelry are, in most cases, some of the accessories most used by women. Banning them would be like the end of the world for many of them. However, too large earrings, as well as many other pieces of jewelry, can be harmful in some cases.

When too large earrings are used, a kind of visual contamination is created. Women with elongated faces will look somewhat *saturated*, while in women with round and wide faces, it will create the illusion of an even bigger and rounded face. Earrings should never be big. The idea is to get a job, not show off your accessories.

The same goes for the rest of your jewelry. If you use a big bracelet or a very large necklace, the image you project is not professional at all.

Imagine for a moment a female senior executive. Imagine her in her executive suit and her black high-heeled shoes. Imagine her blond or brunette. You can even add some glasses to her. Can you imagine her with big and ostentatious jewelry? Surely not.

Now try to imagine her with big earrings, a big bracelet and a very ostentatious necklace. She no longer inspires much confidence and professionalism, right?

I will talk soon about the best options for dress to attend a job interview, but I would like to make something clear before. If you want to use jewelry during your job interview, it's best to follow the main commandment of minimalism—less is more... And more is less.

Sandals, open shoes and sneakers: Shoes are perhaps women's favorite accessories. For women, more than a need, they are a way to show luxury and glamor all the times. Many women invest more money in shoes than in clothes and accessories.

WELCOME ABOARD: MORE THAN 200 TIPS TO MAKE THEM HIRE YOU

Your shoe collection may be the best in the world for you. But like everything else, there are times when it's better to opt for other pieces and not take risks with your personal preferences.

I think there is no need to explain why sport shoes are prohibited. Although they are very practical and comfortable, they are unsightly and informal. If you go to your job interview with sneakers, unless you have a degree from a prestigious university like Harvard, or you are an eminence in your profession, with a great and recognized career, it's better you start to forget that job.

Open shoes are not a good option either. They don't look professional. Also, there is something you should keep in mind. Many employers will look at two things when they observe you—your hands and feet. Bearing that in mind, I doubt very much that you want to show the imperfections of your feet during your first impression.

A few years ago, some plastic clogs in colorful colors became popular. They are very comfortable, it's true. But they will definitely detract from your credibility wherever you go. No need to explain why.

I also don't need to explain why sandals are prohibited too. You go to a job interview, not to the beach nor to an afternoon walk. They are evaluating you. You are not resting or socializing.

Imagine again that executive woman you imagined in the previous point. Imagine her wearing an elegant suit. Now imagine a similar version of her next to—she could be her twin sister. But this other version is wearing a pair of running shoes, open shoes, or a pair of sandals. Which of both of them do you consider that looks more professional and reliable? I think your answer is too obvious for anyone.

Eye-catching prints: Spring designs are almost always full of colorful patterns that are best to avoid. Nowadays, elegance is synonymous with minimalism. And colorful patterns are certainly not elegant at all.

Long-wavelength colors: I will not explain color theory at depth. I will just explain that the colors of a long-wavelength of light, which would be red, pink, yellow and orange, as well as their respective tones—excluding pastel shades—are a bad option when you go to a job interview. They are too intense and don't follow the current canons of elegance.

Usually, red color is culturally interpreted as synonymous with power, desire, lust and sexual innuendo. This perception turns red color into the best option for a first date. But it's not a good option when you are looking for a job. And while it's true that red color, in the vast majority of cultures, indicate strength and power, which makes it an ideal color to demonstrate a certain position, it's not an appropriate color in the dress of any female aspirant.

The red color is the color with the longest wavelength of light, which makes it intensely perceptible. This could make you look more striking and more powerful, so it's a good color to wear when you want to find a partner, apply for a promotion or ask for an increase, but it's not so much when you try to get a job.

When you are looking for a job, it's better to opt for colors that make you look more professional and somewhat more discreet.

However, in case you have to go to a group interview, a touch of red could give you a greater advantage. As people will notice you more by wearing something red, you could have a greater advantage over the rest.

Pink color, on the other hand, will diminish your credibility. Once again, these are cultural stereotypes. When you dress in pink, you have that image of a *spoiled girl*, something that is not favorable at all when you are applying for a job. In addition, most societies associate pink color with lack of power and value, as well as lack of maturity.

When it comes to orange color, the negative response is similar. The orange color is between the range of red and yellow. It's a warm color and very heavy for the eyesight.

Have you noticed that most fast-food chains are orange inside? This is to stimulate your appetite and your desires to leave the restaurant as soon as you finish eating.

The orange color causes this physiological effect. Therefore, when you wear orange at a job interview, you could actually be causing a sense of heaviness in the interviewer, creating a feeling of hunger and craving to end the interview, something that is very negative for any applicant.

Finally, we have the yellow color. Among the long-wavelength colors, this is the color with the shorter wavelength. And although it's the most visually attractive color after red, it still could play against to you.

Yellow color is too bright. This is why it makes some people feel uncomfortable when they watch it for a relatively long time. Some people even say yellow color makes them feel anxiety. As it's a color that reflect too much light, it could be so hard for some people. It's best to avoid it in order to prevent the interviewer from getting uncomfortable.

Jeans: Jeans are very resistant but not very elegant garments. There are also many stereotypes around such versatile garments, which makes them even less elegant.

As they are very comfortable and versatile, many applicants wear jeans when they go to a job interview. And they forget that success to get a job depends on the image they project up to more than 80%.

Very pronounced neckline: In previous chapters we talked about the importance of discretion, as well as the importance of avoiding any possible displays of sexual innuendo. A pronounced neckline is always a synonymous with sexual innuendo. In addition to subtract elegance and sophistication to the set that you wear. Better to avoid any unnecessary risk.

Best clothing options for women

So far I have mentioned what are the most common mistakes in terms of women's clothing when going to a job interview. In this section, I will talk about the best clothing options to get success in your job interview.

These tips can be used in all professions alike. But they are more suitable for executives, administrators, marketing and public relations professionals, accountants, lawyers, publicists, talent agents, managers—practically any economic, administrative or legal profession.

These are the best clothing options for women:

Long-sleeved blouse: Long-sleeved blouses are synonymous with elegance and professionalism. They stylize the silhouette and sometimes, they make you look a little taller and thinner than you are; which translates into an image of elegance, confidence, and power.

There is even a psychological motivation to wear a long-sleeved blouse. When you wear a long-sleeved blouse, it's normal to feel a little more confident. You may even feel and see yourself as a more attractive person. This will immediately rise your level of confidence and allow you to feel more comfortable during your job interview.

Color of the blouse: The color of the blouse you wear during your interview is another important factor to bear in mind. You can use a white blouse or opt for some pastel shade, being sky blue the best option. In most societies, we tend to relate sky blue color with cleanliness, sincerity and serenity.

In previous points, I talked about why you should avoid red, pink, orange and yellow colors. But when it comes to pastel shades, you could make an exception with pink, provided it's a discreet tone and that is easy to combine. Following the same rule, you can also use yellow pastel shades if you want. However, it's best to avoid orange color, even in pastel shades, as isn't easy to combine with other clothes that you will need to create a good impression before the interviewer.

In the same way, as I mentioned, if you had to attend a group interview, you could increase you visibility and your chances of being taken in account by wearing something red. Thus, because red color is the color that has the longest wavelength of light, by wearing something red you will stand out from the crowd. In this case, the white and red combination is a winning option. Both colors combine perfectly, combining the purity, elegance and cleanliness of the white color with the power of the red color. Just make sure that white is the dominant color.

Skirts and dresses in medium length: If you decide to use a skirt or dress to attend your job interview, ideally it should be a medium length. These types of skirts are very discreet and look more professional.

Which color? Well, black or navy blue colors are the best bets. They are easy to combine, very versatile and also stylize the figure.

Stockings: Stockings are the ideal complement if you decide to use a skirt. They add elegance and help to stylize the figure a bit. In addition, they help disguise imperfections in the legs, such as varicose veins, stretch marks or cellulite.

Pants: If your body shape allows you, you can wear dress pants in black or navy blue. This recommendation is up to you. Not all women have the same body or the same height. Use pants only if you think you look good in them.

If you are lucky enough to look good with pants or a skirt alike, use the garment that makes you look taller. Humans, like many other animals, tend to relate height as a synonym of leadership, competitiveness, power, and authority.

Black or navy blue jacket: You can add an extra touch of professionalism and elegance to your wardrobe with a black or navy blue jacket—especially if you are looking for an executive position in a company or as a lawyer.

Some studies have shown that when you wear a jacket you increase your credibility before the people around you. Perhaps that is the reason why all top executives use jackets.

Opt for pearls: When it comes to creating a good first impression, jewelry becomes a minefield. Gold is elegant for some people, but very unsightly and pretentious for others. Diamonds are beautiful but very pretentious. And they could make you look like someone arrogant.

Pearls, on the other hand, are the best option when it comes to jewelry. They are discreet, versatile and combine well with any skin tone.

Pearls are usually complemented perfectly with a jacket in black or navy blue.

Opt for discreet pearl earrings, or if you prefer, a pearl necklace. The important thing is that you remember you should not abuse jewelry, even if they are pearls. Follow the most important rule of minimalism—less is more. Three accessories would be the maximum allowed. Earrings count as an accessory, a necklace is another, and a ring or a watch would be the third. No other accessory is allowed.

High heels: We have already talked about height and how it affects the way we perceive others. Women have a great advantage that men don't have—they can wear high-heeled shoes.

High-heeled shoes can provide you an apparent increase in your height. Too high heels are not a good option, as they could cause you accidents by altering the way you walk.

The best results you get with heels about ten centimeters—four inches. Don't wear shoes with heels more than fifteen centimeters—six inches.

Besides making you look taller, there is a psychological trick behind the use of high heels. When you wear high heels, all the weight of your body falls on the tip of your feet, making your body adopt a more aligned posture, even if you are not aware of it. By adopting a better posture, not only will you be perceived as a more confident person, but you will also feel that way because of the relationship that exist between your posture and the way you feel when you adopt that posture.

Perfume: If you like to use perfume, opt for fresh aromas. Just remember not to abuse on it. Consider perfume as an accessory, not as an article of personal hygiene.

Makeup: Makeup should be considered as an accessory, not as a beauty ritual. With the above in mind, on the day of your interview you should opt for a discreet and natural looking makeup. It's about concealing facial imperfections, not about covering your face with colors.

Most common mistakes in men

Most men tend to have a more limited wardrobe than women. It seems that we men have simpler tastes than women. But unfortunately, many times our fashion sense is even less successful.

Unlike women, who seem obsessed with their appearance, at all times, we men are less aware of our appearance throughout the day. We make sure we look good when we leave home, but we don't really care about our image throughout the day. More importantly, we men, in general, only worry about shaving our face, our hairstyle and that's it.

We generally don't pay attention to our dress style, or at least not in the way we should. We don't usually worry about the combination of colors or shoes. Moreover, in most cases we only pay attention to the shirt or t-shirt we are going to wear. Whatever, a pair of jeans go well with everything.

When we go to a job interview, things are a little more complicated. They are evaluating us every moment. And what we are wearing is one of the points in which more emphasis is made when they are evaluating us. Clothing represents more than 60% of our personal image. And for this reason we should pay more attention to the clothes we use when we go to a job interview.

To not make you wait more, these are the most common dress mistakes in men:

Short-sleeved shirts: Many people think that short-sleeved shirts are a good option—but they are not. Short-sleeved shirts are neither elegant nor formal. They are a good option when we want to keep the style during summer. But they are not a good option when you want to show yourself as the best option to cover a vacancy.

Short-sleeved shirts will not make you look too casual like t-shirts do, but they will not give you formality nor professionalism. It's better to avoid them.

T-shirts: I think it goes without saying why they are not a good option. They are informal, they don't bring elegance nor professionalism. And before the eyes of any recruiter, they make you look like someone immature. Some t-shirt designs are not only informal but also unsightly, specially the sports t-shirts.

Going to a job interview with a sports t-shirt, is not only informal, but also a waste of time.

Nobody cares what your favorite team is or your passion for football, or for any other sport you like. That doesn't interest anyone in the least. And much less to any employer. Employers look for professional people with a desire to excel, not an enthusiast of some sports team.

Believe it or not, I have met more than one person who has gone to a job interview wearing a t-shirt of a football team. Needless to say, they didn't get the job. Is it possible that the way they dressed had something to do with it? I guess the answer is more than obvious.

If your intention is to make a fool of yourself for a moment, inconvenience the people around you and receive unfriendly looks, I recommend you wear your favorite team's t-shirt, go to the stadium and sit in the stands of the opposing team. That way, at least you will not waste any employer's time.

Polo shirts: Polo shirts, also known as golf shirts and tennis shirts, are a good option for an outdoor meal or to enjoy the summer with a touch of elegance, but like short-sleeved shirts, they are not a good option to attend your job interview. Better to avoid them.

Long-wavelength colors: I will not explain color theory at depth. I will only explain that colors of long-wavelength, which would be red, pink, orange, and yellow, as well as all their shades, are a bad option when you go to a job interview. They are too intense and don't follow the current canons of elegance. And unlike women, who can make exceptions with their respective pastel shades, in the case of men, we should refrain from using them during a job interview.

In most western societies, pink color is linked to the feminine. Once again, these are cultural stereotypes. Pink is a very suitable color in a romantic date. Apparently, women see the men who wear in pink as more sensitive, affectionate and tender men. That makes pink color a good option to go out on a first date, but not for a job interview. In addition, pink color is culturally associated with the lack of power and value, as well as the lack of maturity.

What's wrong with orange color? Orange color is between the range of red and yellow. It's a warm color and very heavy for the eyes.

Have you noticed that many fast food chains are orange inside? This is to stimulate your appetite and your desire to leave the restaurant as soon as you finish eating.

Orange color causes this physiological effect. Therefore, when you wear orange at a job interview, you could actually be causing a sense of heaviness in the interviewer, creating a feeling of hunger and craving to end the interview, something that is very negative for any applicant.

There is a small paradox about the red color. Have you noticed that all stop signs are red in any country in the world? This is because the red color is very striking. In fact, it's the color with the longest wavelength of light, And actually, dress in red can be very beneficial on many cases. Dressing in red will make you look more confident, more powerful and even more sexually attractive. It's an ideal color to wear if you want to get a promotion or a salary increase, but you have to be careful when you dress it during a job interview.

Unlike women, in which case it's best to avoid wearing red during a job interview—because red color is culturally linked to sexual innuendo—male applicants can make an exception and wear red color in their favor. I'll talk about it later.

Jeans: They are a favorite for most men. They are very versatile, combine very well with any shirt or t-shirt, are very durable, give us a rough and masculine look, combine well with any kind of shoes, and we can find them in a great variety of styles.

Despite all its advantages, they are not the best option for a job interview since they lack elegance and are very informal. Many companies even prohibit them among their employees during the workday. Better to avoid them.

Sneakers: I don't think it's necessary to say why. But believe it or not, as with sports t-shirts, I've met several people who have worn sports shoes during a job interview.

Sneakers, like jeans, are pretty comfortable and versatile, but they are not the best option when we want to create a good first impression.

One of the things employers—and most people—observe when they meet someone for the first time are shoes. Supposedly, that way you can better know the person, or at least their purchasing power and their concern of their appearance. It's simple, avoid sneakers.

Leather jackets: Leather jackets are used by motorcyclists to avoid serious scratches and chafing when an accident happens. But the entertainment industry sold us the image of the bad boy on a motorcycle—that boy who always gets the girls, always wearing a leather jacket. That image made many men consider leather jackets as a way to look rough and interesting.

In previous chapters we talked about the apparent image. And while a leather jacket can make you look like a rough and interesting man before some people, it also can generates another apparent image, the image of an aggressive and possibly violent person.

If you want to get a job in a company, the last thing you want is to be perceived as a violent person or worse, as a criminal.

Remember that stereotypes are the basis of the judgements of most people. Bearing this in mind, it boils down to a simple recommendation—avoid leather jackets.

Using a suit jacket without a tie: A common mistake when it comes to wearing a suit jacket is to forget—or to decide not to wear—the tie. When you wear a suit without a tie, most people, including employers, recruiters and interviewers, will perceive the attire as incomplete. This can negatively affect the perception that interviewers get from you.

First of all, if you dress in an *incomplete* manner, the interviewer may think that you are unable to complete certain tasks and therefore, you won't have a good performance within the company. Also remember that the first impression is a key element to get the job or not.

White socks: White socks are a good option when we choose to wear sports clothes, but they are not when we want to look elegant and professional. They are too unsightly when used with dress pants, especially when combined with black, navy blue, gray, brown or beige pants.

Jewelry: Some men use jewelry thinking this way they would demonstrate a better purchasing power and thus to appear to be in a better social position.

While it's true that certain metals such as gold and silver are highly coveted for their scarcity, it's also true that they are very unsightly for some people. And certainly, jewelry in men lacks elegance in most cases.

In a few words, don't wear jewelry the day of your interview. The only exception would be your wedding ring, if you are married. No bracelets, chains, nor graduation rings.

Best clothing options for men

So far I have mentioned what are the most common mistakes in clothing in men during a job interview. In this section I will talk about the best clothing options to be successful in your job interview.

These tips can be used in all professions alike. But they are more suitable for executives, administrators, marketing and public relations professionals, accountants, lawyers, publicists, talent agents, managers—practically any economic, administrative or legal profession.

These are the best clothing options for men:

Long-sleeved shirts: Long-sleeved shirts are the best option we can choose when we try to dress elegantly and definitely, they are also a good option to wear during your job interview.

Long-sleeved shirts sends a message of professionalism, education, elegance and responsibility—qualities any employer seeks.

Color of the shirt: Although long-sleeved shirts are a safe bet in your outfit, there are some shades that can make you look like a more attractive candidate—blue and white.

In western culture, blue color communicates elegance, professionalism and sincerity. This is the reason why some lawyers suggest their clients wear a blue shirt or a blue tie during the trial. This way, they could persuade the jury and thus avoid a possible conviction, or at least a reduction of it.

There is also a scientific trick behind this color. Blue color, especially sky blue shade, create a chemical reaction in our brains that relaxes us and puts us in a good mood. That would explain why we feel in a better mood on a sunny day with clear skies, while we feel less happy and possibly depressed during rainy days. And when you dress in blue, especially in azure shades, people can experience some relaxation in your presence.

Personally, I have noticed that I get a better treatment of people when I dress sky blue shirts, I guess it's due to the chemical reaction in the brain that neuroscientists talk about.

White color, on the other hand, is widely used in the business world. It communicates elegance, professionalism, efficiency and cleanliness. It's a classic that, due to its versatility, never goes out of style.

Suit: A suit is definitely the most elegant piece that a man can have in his wardrobe. A good suit will not only make you look more elegant, but also, even if you don't believe it, it will give you a little more respect from others.

Many people say they feel more confident when they wear suits. But they don't realize that their body language, especially their posture, changes when they wear a suit. That change in their body language is what make them feel more confident, at the same time they are perceived as trusting people and therefore, people around them treat them better.

Suit color: Although a suit seems to be a fault-free option, it's necessary to take certain precautions, especially on color.

There are three good color options to wear during a job interview—navy blue, gray, and black.

A navy blue suit is a very current option. It's not so serious, but not so daring either. When we talk about a navy blue suit, we are talking about a dark navy blue suit. There are some suits in lighter navy blue shades, which are better to avoid. The navy blue color is the best choice for men with a light skin tone.

Gray suits seem to be very requested nowadays. It looks contemporary, fresh and adds a youthful touch, at the same time that it seems sober and discreet. Of the three colors mentioned above, it's the best choice for men with olive or dark skin.

Finally, the black suit is a classic that doesn't go out of style. And although many people currently find it somewhat boring and outdated, a black suit is still a good option. It goes well with any skin tone, accentuates light skin tones and softens dark skin tones. In addition, it blends perfectly with any shirt color.

Discreet ties: I recommend you use discreet ties, either solid color or very discreet designs. Avoid saturated designs. You will want them see you, not your tie.

Your face should be remembered to increase your chances of being hired.

Do you remember that I mentioned that men can use red color in their favor during a job interview? The red color is culturally interpreted throughout the world as synonymous with strength and power. For this reason, discreetly wearing the red color during a job interview, by using a red tie, for example, can increase your chances of looking more confident and powerful.

Red ties combine perfectly with light colored shirts—especially with white and sky blue colors. If you are an observer person, you will have noticed that many politicians often wear red ties when they wear white or sky blue shirts. And the reason why many politicians often wear red ties is because the red color communicates leadership, strength and power. In the same way, red color is the color with the longest wavelength, which turns the red color in the most striking and visible color to the eyes.

Cufflinks: Cufflinks, along with the engagement ring and an elegant, discreet watch, are the only type of jewelry allowed during a job interview or in any other occasion where to dress elegantly be crucial.

Cufflinks are a kind of accessory for long-sleeved shirts. They offer elegance and sophistication. Well used, they will make you look more sophisticated and important. Remember, the image is the most important thing.

Socks in black, navy blue or gray: Choose the color of your socks according on the suit color you choose. Many men make the mistake of wearing brown or beige socks with black suits. I've even seen some men wear white socks, believe it or not, with black pants. That's not only unsightly, but also shows your lack of attention to details, which is crucial in many jobs.

Leather shoes in black: Choose a pair of black leather shoes to attend your interview. It's true that brown shoes can look good with gray and sometimes, with blue pants. But it's best to avoid unnecessary risks.

Brown shoes look good on many occasions. But they are not the best option for a job interview. Your appearance should be elegant, sober and discreet.

Choose to wear black shoes, regardless of the color of your suit. Black shoes combine perfectly with pants in navy blue, gray and black alike. They are a safe bet.

Lotion: The most recommended lotions are those that have citrus aromas. Just don't overuse it. Use it with discretion.

Is it necessary to dress in the ways mentioned above?

It's highly recommended.

Mistakes in clothing are universal, while the aforementioned dress tips can be used by any applicant, regardless of their profession. However, they are more oriented to professionals in financial or legal world, such as marketing, administration, accounting, public relations, advertising, sales, law, senior management and others.

Regardless of your profession, the same tips will be useful, but you may also feel like a fish out of the water, especially if you practice a creative profession sus as graphic design, music, or photography; in which case, wearing a suit might be seen a little exaggerated. It's also possible that you live in a very warm place. In these cases, is it possible to change the *right* way of dressing a bit?

The answer is yes. But remember that is perhaps the most important element during a job interview. The more elegant you look, the more chances there are of getting the job. You can do without the jacket, using a long-sleeved or a 3/4 sleeve blouse in white or pastel shades in case of women. Or long-sleeved shirts in sky blue or white in the case of men.

You can choose another type of dress if you wish. That is your decision. But the best would be to take the advice I have mentioned above.

Remember that the image you show will be one of the points that will matter most to the interviewer. So a good appearance will increase your chances of getting the job. Under no circumstances wear sneakers, sandals, t-shirts or jewelry.

Summary of how to dress to get hired

- Remember that the image you project influences in the employer's decision by more than 60%.

- A good resume could get overshadowed by the bad image of the applicant.

- If you're a woman, avoid wearing short skirts; oversized earrings and jewelry; sandals; open shoes and sneakers; garments with colorful prints; garments in red—unless you attend a group interview—pink and orange; very pronounced cleavage; and jeans.

- If you're a man, avoid wearing short-sleeved shirts; T-shirts; polo shirts; garments in red—although ties in red can give you a greater advantage—pink and orange; sneakers; suit without tie; jewelry; leather jackets; jeans; and white socks.

- If you're a woman, choose to wear a long-sleeved blouse in white or pastel shades; skirts and dresses of medium length; stockings; pants; black or navy blue jacket; high heels; fresh scent perfume; discreet makeup; and if you want to wear jewelry, choose to wear pearls, both in earrings and necklaces.

- If you're a man, choose to wear long-sleeve shirts in sky blue or white; a suit in navy blue, gray or black; citric essence lotion; ties with discreet designs, if matches with your outfit, better in red; cufflinks; socks in black, navy blue or gray, according on your suit color; and black shoes.

- If you don't feel comfortable with the aforementioned outfits, you can do without the jacket, using a long-sleeve or 3/4 sleeve blouse in white or pastel shades in case of women; or a long-sleeved shirt in sky blue or white in the case of men.

- You can choose any other type of clothing if you want, just be aware of the image you project. Remember that the image you project is very important if you want to get a job within a company.

Tips for the big day

If you got to this point, I suppose that by now you will have noticed some mistakes that you may have made in the past. I imagine your resume has already been polished and it's even more attractive than before. You already know how powerful the image, the appearance and the attitude of the aspirants can be in the employer's final decision. You even know that it can be even more important than your resume itself.

You have learned about your body language and the message it conveys, even without saying a single word. You learned to read your recruiter's body language and to use persuasion in your favor. You learned how to write a cover letter, and I suppose if you've already made one, it's probably very attractive. I imagine you have already done a research about the company you wish to belong to. And finally, I guess you already know how you'll dress the day of your interview.

I recommend you continue reviewing each summary of each chapter in order to increase your possibilities to get that job. Even so, there are some other tips that may be useful for you on the day of your interview.

In this chapter I'll show you some tips that will help you feel more confident and some other tips that will be helpful to eliminate stress and insecurity.

Don't forget your appointment

What would happen if you forget the date and time of your appointment and then ask to be assigned another? Well, it's very difficult to get another appointment.

The reason is simple. You have already created an image of irresponsibility and lack of interest.

When you confirm the date of your appointment for the interview, don't forget to schedule it.

Traditional appointment books have a flaw—you have to check them constantly. I don't recommend them at all, since by generating a dependency to check them you could slightly increase your stress levels. And although it's also true that many studies have shown that handwriting, unlike typing, helps keeping things on our memory, you may forget to check your appointment book.

I know some people who, despite having scheduled their appointment in an appointment book, confused the day of their interviews. This happened to an acquaintance of mine. He scheduled his appointment for a Tuesday, but despite remembering the date, he believed that that date was a Wednesday. That Wednesday, believing it was the correct date, he got ready for his interview, took his appointment book, looked at the screen of his mobile phone to check the date and realized that the appointment was the previous day.

Traditional appointment books are excellent when we maintain certain constancy and discipline in our habits. But sometimes, especially when we don't follow a routine, notifications are very useful to remember our to-dos.

Currently, all mobile phones, computers and tablets have calendar applications that remind you of the events you have added through notifications. There are even applications that can synchronize your calendar between your phone, your computer, and your tablet. This way, chances of forgetting your appointment are almost nil.

I recommend you add three annotations with alarm in your calendar app. The first would be with the date and time of your appointment, with a lapse of time prior to your appointment time between one or two hours, maybe more, depending on the distance between your home and the company. This way, you will have enough time to groom, get dressed, and take breakfast.

Many people consider that taking breakfast is not important. And that's a very serious mistake. When you don't take breakfast, your brain is deprived of glucose, which is necessary to perform many cognitive functions. In short, if you don't take breakfast, you will be—and you will look—anxious and agitated.

The second entry would be one day in advance of your interview, between seven and nine in the evening. This annotation will serve to give you the opportunity to finish your day early and go to bed as early as possible.

The day of your interview you should look relaxed and rested. If you don't sleep well, you will have dark circles, which you like or not, are part of the image you project. A person who looks tired tends to generate an image of boredom, incompetence and lack of interest. You don't want to give that impression, right?

The third entry would be two days prior your appointment. This way, you can have all your documents ready a few days in advance. Don't wait until the last minute to prepare your documents. Have your portfolio ready two days in advance.

Organize everything at least two days in advance

The day of your interview you will be a little nervous, which is very normal. Nerves cloud our mind, so to speak.

Has it happened to you that when you look for an object you never find it, but when the same object doesn't interest you anymore, it appears before your eyes at all times? In fact, the object was always in the same place. But stress *hid it* from your sight, so to speak. It's very likely that the same thing will happen to you on the day of your interview. You won't want to be late and because of that, your mind will focus on the most important things at that moment, leaving everything else out of your working memory.

As I already suggested, organize everything you need at least two days in advance. Keep in the portfolio all those documents that you will take to your interview and place the portfolio in a visible place so you won't forget it.

Remember to take several copies of your resume with you, with the best possible presentation, as well as copies of your reference lists. And if your profile requires it, as in the case of professionals in advertising, graphic design, illustration, and photography, organize a professional portfolio with which you can demonstrate your skills and previous works.

Choose your clothes and shoes the night before your interview. If necessary to polish your shoes, do it the night before. The same goes for your clothes. Choose the clothes you will wear during your interview the night before and have them ready to get ready the next morning. Choose everything that you will need with at least one night in advance, so that on the day of your appointment you should only focus on the interview.

Sleep well

In previous recommendations I suggested you to schedule a reminder in your calendar app one night before your appointment, so you can go to bed early that night. Actually, my recommendation is as follows, start sleeping early at least three days in advance. Otherwise, you will not be able to go to sleep early the night prior your interview.

You may think that getting a good night's sleep is not a priority for you. But when you look tired, people think you're bored, indecisive, clumsy, and lacking in optimism. Do you really want to give that image to the employer?

Have breakfast before going to your interview

As I mentioned in other sections of this book, many people decide to do without breakfast to *save* time. This is one of the worst decisions you can make. When we skip breakfast, we deprive our brain of the glucose it needs for cognitive functions. In other words, tasks as simple as answering a series of questions, can be hindered by the lack of glucose in the brain, that is, by skipping breakfast.

Almost no one imagines this recommendation would appear in a book like this one—a book whose main propose is to secure the obtaining of a job. But this is one of the most common mistakes many aspirants make.

Not all breakfast work the same way. All of them take away your hunger at the moment, but some of them can cause heartburn or flatulence. Others may leave you satisfied for a moment, but hunger return in less than half an hour.

I want to explain you how the ideal breakfast should be and what are the biggest mistakes when it comes to breakfast.

Breakfast should include protein. Proteins will give you energy and will keep you satisfied longer. Eggs, fish, some chicken or lean meat are the best options.

As a drink, include tea, of any kind. Many people confuse tea with the rest of infusions. Te is an infusion made from the leaf of the tea plant—Camellia Sinesis—and its best-known varieties are black tea, green tea, and white tea.

You can choose any of the varieties of tea. If you are used to drinking coffee, you can opt for black tea. Conversely, if caffeine is contraindicated, it's better to opt for white tea, which has very low levels of caffeine. Green tea is a neutral point between black tea and white tea in terms of its caffeine level. The most important thing is that you drink the tea without any additive, especially dairy products. If you are not used to the taste of tea, you can add some sweetener, being honey, if not contraindicated, the most recommended option.

Avoid coffee and milk.

You may be wondering, why should not I drink coffee or milk? And maybe you may also be wondering, why do you recommend drinking tea that day?

First, I'll explain why I recommend drinking tea on the day of your interview. Tea has low levels of caffeine, which will keep you alert but not anxious. In addition, it contains some substances that improve concentration and reduce stress—a benefit that coffee doesn't offer.

On the contrary, coffee will keep you alert, it's true. But it will also keep you anxious. And if you have some kind of nervous tic, the high levels of caffeine in coffee could make it worse. I just wouldn't recommend it.

On the other hand, more than 60% of the population suffer from some type of intolerance to dairy products and don't know it, which can cause them problems of flatulence, abdominal pain, feeling of disgust, desire to vomit, and in the worst case, diarrhea.

The milk also contains tryptophan, an amino acid capable of making us feel good. But not all are good news. Tryptophan can relax us too much, reaching the edge of drowsiness. That's the reason why many people drink milk before going to sleep. Just like coffee, I wouldn't recommend it.

If you want to consume fruit, do it ten minutes before consuming protein. Otherwise, the chances of flatulence after half an hour could be high.

I would not recommend breakfast cereals, toast with jelly, nor industrial bakery at all. They will satisfy you for a few minutes, but after twenty minutes your body will begin to feel hungry again, which means that you will begin to feel anxious in a few minutes.

Remove dark circles

Dark circles make you look tired and even sick. That would ruin the image you want to project. Instead of making a happy and youthful impression, the impression you will make on others will be that of someone bored and unfriendly.

Spending nights without sleep, or not getting enough sleep, causes those discomforts dark marks around the eyes.

One of the recommendations I have given you is to get a good night's sleep before your appointment. If for some reason those dark circles persist around your eyes, it's better to disguise them.

There are some cosmetic products that help to hide dark circles. But if you don't have any commercial products at hand, there are some natural alternatives that you can use.

If you drank black tea or green tea at breakfast, you can put the tea bag for a few minutes in the freezer. Once it has cooled, lightly press on the dark circles with the tea bag.

If you drank white tea, or if the dark circles are very intense, make a very concentrate coffee. Not too much, 15 or 20 milliliters—around 3 teaspoons or 1 tablespoon—will be enough. Once you have made the coffee, add ice and shake it to cool it. Remove the ice and soak a piece of cotton into the iced coffee. Then, wipe the moistened cotton around your eyes. Caffeine helps improving blood circulation around your eyes, and cold has an anti-inflammatory effect. This should be enough to disguise your dark circles.

Make sure you arrive on time.

I recommend you arrive at least 20 minutes before your interview. Nowadays, punctuality is very scarce and therefore, more valued than ever. Companies look for punctual and responsible people. That's the image you must to show from the first day.

There may be too many unforeseen events, such as car accidents that slow down traffic, protests, repairs on public roads, and many other eventualities that could hinder your intentions to arrive on time.

Make sure you arrive 20 minutes before your appointment, but don't advertise yourself until five minutes before your interview. Those 20 minutes should not be considered as lost time.

Next, I'll give you some tips to make better use of those 20 minutes.

Just relax

If you arrive 20 minutes before your appointment, you get two advantages. First of all you will be perceived as a punctual and responsible aspirant. The other advantage has to do with an additional advantage—you have time to relax.

When you are in a job interview, it's normal that nerves attack you. But during the next 20 minutes you can try to reduce your stress levels.

During the next 20 minutes prior to your interview, you only have to pay attention to your breathing. Something like meditating, but with your eyes open. If you meditate in a waiting room, you may look tired and sleepy. But by paying attention to your breathing, you will get the same benefits that you would get with a meditation session. In other words, you will look relaxed and confident.

You can also read a book or a magazine, and even interact with the people around you, but you need to pay attention on your breathing at all times.

Breath in and breath out. And during that process, be aware of it.

If you think that staying focused on your breathing may be very difficult for you, start practicing this technique the next time you talk to someone.

You could be observed

Most companies have security cameras in their waiting areas, but that is not what should worry you. Some companies uses cameras to analyze the behavior of the applicants. That should matter to you, but don't worry.

Review the chapters in which I speak about the image and body language. This way, if your behavior is analyzed in secret, you will have nothing to worry about. On the contrary, you will have some extra points in your favor.

Certainly, there is no way to know if the company you want to belong to will analyze your behavior, but you should assume they will. If you suffer from nervous tics, try to eliminate them. Keeping focused on your breathing is very useful to eliminate, or at least reduce, those nervous tics.

Avoid eating your nails, playing with your hair, whistling, playing with your hands, smoking, scratching unnecessarily, and any other behavior that may be *unpleasant* for others.

Be kind and don't argue

Imagine the next scene:

You enter the company's building. You show up at the reception, and the receptionist tells you in a rude tone: "Do you mind? I'm busy!"

How would you react?

More than half of the population will react in the same way. They would rise their voice tone, frown and respond in an equally rude manner.

Is it really worth it to retaliate?

Remember that some companies use cameras to evaluate the applicants behavior. It's not worth taking any risk. It's possible that the receptionist, or anyone who answers you in an unfriendly manner, is going through some bad time. And at that moment, you were the only person whom she could retaliate.

It's not your fault. I know. But it's no use putting you on the defensive. You would only make a bad impression on the people around you, starting with the human resources staff.

The best thing is to forget that incident, swallow your pride and continue as if nothing had happened. If someone responds to you in an unpleasant way, simply respond with a smile, saying something like, "Excuse me if I caused you any discomfort. Have a nice day." Then, retire as if nothing had happened, with your head held high and walking at a speed a little slower than usual—without any haste.

You could receive an apology, although it's most likely not the case. Just forget that incident and concentrate on your breathing. It will help you relax and dissolve anger.

If after that episode you think your pride has been crushed, it will comfort you to know that psychologically, people who shout at someone and receive a kind treatment from the person they have shouted, tend to feel guilty and may even see themselves as idiots during the following minutes to the incident.

Make yourself noticed and get others to take you into account

It's useless to have good credentials and dress elegantly if you pass unnoticed.

In previous chapters I talked about leadership and submission. Leaders are noted, while the submissive people, on the other hand, retreat and try to pass unnoticed.

Act as a leader and you will be noticed immediately.

When people make themselves noticed, they tend to be remembered. And if people remember you, your networking gets bigger and more useful for the future. It's not time to be antisocial, much less unfriendly to any person within the company.

All of the people within the company can be in some way useful for you to get that job you want. And once you reach certain position within the company, your social relationships and the sympathy that you have generated before others, will be useful when you look for a better position within the company,

When you enter the company's building, walk with your head up, taking care of your posture at all times. Walk a little slower than usual, as if you were on a fashion runway. And say hello to everyone you meet.

A simple phrase like "good morning," accompanied with a smile, will not only have a strong impact on the people you addressing, but it will also have an impact on you. Without realizing it, your level of confidence will increase.

When you go to the waiting room, locate yourself in the center of it. Self-confident people like to be observed and admired, while shy and submissive people tend to sit in corners to go unnoticed. People who are most visible are the most remembered and generally, they get the best jobs and the best salaries.

Making yourself noticed and socializing will not only help you get a job. Getting a job doesn't mean you will get a job for life. The cuts of personnel are increasingly common in a world of crisis. And those who demonstrate greater social skills are less vulnerable to a personnel cut. If you are able to make yourself known to other members of the company, people will have a good image of you. That means that your superiors will consider why you should remain in the organization if there were any cuts in personnel.

Remember that you have to make yourself noticed, otherwise you will show yourself as someone who is unable to socialize. But there is something that I want you to take into account. Being social doesn't mean bothering someone who is not interested in any conversation or your company, nor does it means being with a person all day long without letting him take a breath. There is a very thin line between being a social and friendly person, and being an annoying person.

There are some people who try to capture the attention of others. In their mind, they believe they are social and friendly people. However, the results they get are totally opposite. As a general rule, if you notice that you bother someone, it may be a problem of that particular person. But if you notice that you are bothering the majority, it means the problem lies with you. In that case, my best advice is to try to change that aspect of you. Once you do it, your life will change for the better.

If you are able to socialize with people around you and your behavior is secretly analyzed, you would be showing yourself as a person who is capable of working as a team—something that companies value a lot today.

Summary of Tips for the big day

- Use the calendar application of your mobile phone to remember your appointment.

- Organize everything you need at least two days in advance.

- Remember to take several copies of your resume with you, with the best possible presentation.

- Choose your clothes and shoes at least one night in advance.

- Sleep well the night before. You will avoid dark circles and other signs of fatigue.

- Have breakfast before going to your appointment. Make sure you include proteins so you don't feel hungry within a few hours.

- Drink tea instead of coffee. Avoid drinking milk.

- Make sure you don't have dark circles.

- Arrive at your appointment 20 minutes in advance, but not advertise yourself until five minutes before your appointment.

- During the waiting minutes prior your interview, focus on your breathing. It will help you relax and release nerves.

- Some companies use cameras to analyze the behavior of their potential candidates. Use that resource in your favor.

- When you go to the waiting room, locate yourself in the center to make yourself noticed.

- Be kind at all times. Don't argue with anyone.

- Make yourself noticed and try to socialize.

Tips to succeed in your interview

Everything you have read in previous chapters will have a strong impact on your interview.

A good cover letter guarantees that your resume will be read.

A well-written resume will allow you to get an appointment for a job interview.

Your image, your attitude and your body language will make you able to make an excellent first impression.

But the final word will be said in your interview.

Your interview is that crucial moment. During your interview, you must be able to show that you are the best option for them at that time. It's the moment in which your possible employer will be impressed or disinterested by you. It's the time at which you may or may not get the job. It's definitely the crucial moment to get the job.

In this chapter, I'll give you some tips to be able to stand out during your interview. Tips that will help you stand out from the rest of the applicants and help you increase your chances of getting hired.

Turn off any mobile device

No kidding.

Currently, mobile phones allow us to be closer to those who are farther away. But at the same time, they separate us from the people we have near.

Nowadays it's very common to see people ignoring others for writing messages on their mobile devices. This type of people claims to be writing and listening at the same time, but they generally ignore the person who is speaking with them—the person who, unlike the person who will receive the text, is next to them at that moment.

There is nothing more annoying for a person than being ignored. Still, many people like to feel important by writing texts on their mobile devices. It makes them feel that, in some way, they are showing to others that they have a long networking. And what actually happens is that, while you ignore those people who are giving you their time, you are losing the sympathy of them. And certainly, no one will care about your supposed networking.

Your friends and family could tolerate it, but the interviewer will never forgive you for ignoring him. You will never have a second chance to make a good first impression. And certainly, being texting will make them think your are a person who doesn't take things seriously. And therefore, you aren't really interested in employment.

There is nothing more annoying for anyone, especially for an interviewer, that being talking to someone and to be interrupted with a phrase like, "Excuse me for a moment. I just answer a message."

Nobody likes to be ignored and if you do it, the only result you will get will be negative. You will automatically be perceived as someone who is not interested in the job. Is it worth the risk?

Turn off any mobile device that you bring with you before entering your interview—tablets, mobile phones, laptops, music players, smart watches and all those mobile devices that are capable of receiving notifications.

Turn them off. Don't use the airplane mode nor put them on vibrator mode.

Believe it or not, many people get anxiety when they leave their homes without their mobile phones. Something similar happens when they receive a message and can't answer—signs of stress and anxiety begin to appear. And if you remember the chapters of image and body language, you should remember that you should avoid any sign of stress or anxiety.

If you turn off all of your mobile devices, mainly your mobile phone, you will not have the need to place it on the desk. There are some studies that show that placing the mobile phone on the table is harmful to your image on a first date. And obviously, the same thing happens during a job interview. Not only is it unprofessional, but the interviewer may be tempted to look at your phone instead of paying attention to you. Keep your phone away from the sight of anyone. This way, they can only concentrate on you.

Be friendly and cordial

When you introduce yourself to the interviewer, smile and say hello with courtesy.

Be the first to shake hands. This way you can keep eye contact when the interviewer shakes your hand. If you are a man and the person conducting the interview is a woman, don't shake her hand unless she does it first. Avoid kisses, regardless of your sex or the sex of the interviewer. It's a job interview, not a date. Don't touch the interviewer unnecessarily, otherwise you will look like a somewhat daring person.

Introduce yourself to the interviewer and don't forget to ask, "How are you?" Believe it or not, a simple question like that generates a better predisposition. We all like to feel important, and when someone shows us a genuine and disinterested interest, our predisposition towards the other person tends to be positive. Use this resource in your favor to get sympathy.

Take a seat only when the interviewer tells you to. This way you will show yourself as a polite and elegant person, besides giving the impression that you know how to respect hierarchies.

Thirty-seconds speech

If you got a job interview, it would be because your cover letter and resume impressed the employer. Now it's time to show that your resume doesn't lie. Have ready a thirty-seconds speech to convince the interviewer that your resume really reflects what you can do for the company.

Prepare your speech a few days in advance. It's not necessary that you recite it by heart, but you should be able to remember the most important points—those that will convince the interviewer that you are the one who deserves the job.

Mention first those qualities that make you stand out. That is, mention positive things before negative ones. The reason for this point is simple. When we listen to a speech, after a while our brain goes on *automatic pilot,* so to speak. That means that the interviewer, while remaining attentive to your entire speech, will only be able to stay fully focused on the first few key words.

I'll give you an example. Pay attention to the bold text.

"I have a degree in business administration, and I have worked for two hotel chains. **I'm an organized and efficient person. I speak fluent Spanish and French, and I like to work with people. But I'm also a little bit authoritarian and I tend to be too perfectionist at times.**"

Now let's look at the same example but with the negative aspects at the beginning.

"I have a degree in business administration, and I have worked for two hotel chains. **I'm a bit authoritarian and I tend to be too perfectionist at times. But I'm also an organized and efficient person. I speak fluent Spanish and French, and I like to work with people.**"

As you can see, the message doesn't vary at all. In both examples, the applicant expressed the same message. But even if it's hard to believe, the first example would be more efficient.

If you want your speech to be efficient, say first those positive points and then those aspects in which it's necessary to work.

If you are thinking of pronouncing the positive aspects only and avoiding the negative ones in order to secure your position in the company, I have bad news for you.

A person who only has positive aspects falls in the *too good to be true* category. But by mentioning some negative qualities, and making the employer see that you are working on them and they wont' be an obstacle to your professional development, they will get a better image of you.

One last clarification. When I ask you to make a thirty-seconds speech, I mean you make a speech that can exemplify your best qualities in that period of time. Don't pretend to elaborate a great speech during that small lapse of time. That is, don't elaborate a speech that forces you to talk fast. Your speech should last thirty seconds or so, but you should appear calm, confident, and elegant when speaking.

Don't show yourself desperate for the job

Avoid looking as someone who is desperate to get the job. Otherwise, the interviewer may think that you want the job only for the salary. Although, being honest, it's most likely so.

Remember that companies don't look for unemployed people that they can support financially. Companies are looking for people that can help them to increase their productivity and income. If you show yourself as someone desperate to find a job, it will be obvious that you don't want to contribute anything to the company. And in that case, they will prefer someone else.

Act naturally, as if you had other options in case you don't get that job. But don't show yourself indifferent to the job either, as if you didn't care.

Remember, it's a personal sale

When you go to a job interview, you're really trying to sell yourself as if you were a product in the supermarket. There are many other options out there waiting for the same job, so you must show that you are the best option to them. For this, your attitude must be positive and you must be able to promote your achievements.

It's not time to be shy and submissive. It's not time to be humble when talking about your achievements, If you don't sell yourself properly, another aspirant will do so and he will get that job you didn't manage to occupy. Speak about your achievements with confidence and a positive attitude.

Keep eye contact

Make sure you keep eye contact during your interview. Keeping eye contact is a sign of confidence and leadership.

Make sure you look away for a few moments. For example, when you have to show your resume, you can watch it for a few seconds. The idea is keeping eye contact, but not so much like a hostile person. I have talked about this topic in other chapters, which I recommend you to review again if necessary.

Posture and body language

In other chapters, I have talked about posture and body language. But as a review, and concentrating on you interview, I'll leave you some additional tips.

Watch your posture when standing. Stay upright and don't walk in a hurry. You will seem self-confident to others.

When you sit down, recharge your back on the backrest. Not only will you feel more comfortable, but you will also show a more confident posture. Keep your shoulders up and avoid seeming hunched. Tilt your torso slightly towards the interviewer to show more interest.

Make sure your feet tough the ground completely. That will be enough to control any nervous movements of your legs. Make sure you don't cross your legs or your feet. Try also to avoid nervous tics, such as moving your feet, legs, or drumming your fingers on the table.

Finally, make sure to keep your hands always visible on the desk. Otherwise, the interviewer may consider that you are hiding something, which will cause mistrust.

Avoid tics

If you have nervous tics, try to eliminate them. Eating your nails, playing with your hair, drumming your fingers on the table, playing with your hands, scratching unnecessarily, making noises, whistling, singing, moving your feet, and any other *bad behavior* should be avoided. Not only is it annoying, but you could also be perceived as an incompetent person.

Don't interrupt the interviewer

Never interrupt the interviewer when he is talking. If you are one of those people who are always interrupting others because they want to express what they think, get used to waiting a couple of seconds before say something.

Listen carefully to what the interviewer says, but make him understand that you are paying attention. Nod slightly to let him know you are paying attention.

At the end of the interview

When the interview is over, stand up and thank the interviewer for granting you the opportunity to be interviewed.

Say goodbye with a firm handshake, keeping eye contact, and smiling.

When leaving the office, be aware of your posture. Make sure you have not stooped. Also make sure you leave the office relaxed and unhurried. And keep an upright posture at all times.

Summary of Tips to succeed in your interview

- Turn off any mobile device before entering your interview.

- Be kind and cordial.

- Be the first to shake hands when you say hello. This way you will keep eye contact during the handshake.

- If you are a man and the person conducting the interview is a woman, don't shake her hand unless she does it first.

- Never greet the interviewer with kisses. Don't touch him unnecessarily either.

- When you introduce yourself to the interviewer, ask him a question like, "How are you?" or something similar.

- Don't take a seat until the interviewer tells you to.

- Make a thirty-seconds speech.

- During your thirty-seconds speech, first mention your positive qualities and finally the negative ones.

- Don't show yourself desperate to get the job.

- Remember that a job interview is a personal sale.

- Show yourself as someone confident and don't be shy when mentioning your achievements.

- Keep eye contact during your interview.

- Keep an upright posture when standing.

- Don't walk in a hurry.

- When sitting down, recharge your back on the backrest of the seat and make sure your feet touch the floor completely.

- Keep your hands visible during the interview.

- Avoid any kind of nervous tic or any other *bad behavior.*

- Never interrupt the interviewer when he is talking.

- Listen carefully to the interviewer and nod your head to let him know you are paying attention.

- At the end of the interview, stand up and thank the interviewer.

- Say goodbye to the interviewer with a firm handshake, keeping eye contact and smiling.

- When you're leaving the office, be sure your posture is still upright and walk without haste.

Most common questions during a job interview

It's impossible to know which questions will be asked during a job interview. Recruiters don't use a standardized questionnaire.

Even so, there is a series of questions that seem to be universal. These are questions that, in some way, have become the norm in most companies. I'm not suggesting these will be the questions they will ask you during your interview. But there is a good chance that they will ask you one or more of those questions.

In this chapter I'll include some of the most common questions asked during a job interview. The questions I will explain below come from two sources: my own personal experience and from the recruiters I interviewed.

With a quick search on the internet, it's possible to find more examples of possible questions that recruiters can ask you during a job interview, which have been written by several recruiters, or by users who have gone through that experience. I don't include them in this book because those examples were not written by me and therefore, I don't own the rights to publish them. But if you decide to review those questions, a quick search on the web will give you the most relevant results in a few seconds.

Below, I'll explain what are the most common questions, along with a series of recommendation to answer them.

Tell me about yourself: It's not a question itself. Rather it's a way to break the ice and start the interview. It's the best time to recite your thirty-seconds speech. It's time to impress the recruiter and make him want to know more about you.

Expose your education background and your most relevant achievements according to the profile of the company and the job you are looking for; as well as the main reason why you want that job.

Why are you interested in working with us?: This question is very common, and I can almost assure you that they will ask it you. There is a chapter in where I talk about the importance of knowing the company. You can answer this question according to the information you got about the company and the job you are looking for.

Why did you quit your previous job?: A difficult question for many people. It's basically a way to look for weaknesses in the aspirants. They will hardly hire someone who speaks ill of their previous bosses or of the company for which they worked. That would indicate disloyalty, something that is not very favorable for any company.

Why are you thinking about quitting your current job?: If you already have a job and are looking for a job in another company, it's normal that recruiters have some doubts about. Answer with sincerity, without speaking ill of the company for which you are currently working.

You can say that you are looking for another job because you want to grow in your career, or because you think you need to move on another company in order to improve your skills and your knowledge.

Any reason to change a job is valid. Just be honest. And don't mention anything about money.

Tell me about your previous boss: Very similar to the last question. It's likely that it's a question to know your level of loyalty to the company. Whatever your answer is, speak as best you can about your previous boss. As with your thirty-seconds speech, expose first the positive qualities of your previous boss and then the negative ones.

It's normal to have problems with the bosses sometimes. We can't agree them all the time. Many people say that their bosses are looking for problems and abuse their authority. But all people have strengths and weaknesses. You must be intelligent when answering these types of questions so as not to generate a bad image of yourself.

If you had a very strict and demanding boss, why say that he was demanding, strict and bad person. Instead, better say he was a perfectionist and that thanks to that, he usually gets good results.

Don't speak badly of your previous boss. Even if there was some kind of resentment, try to analyze what his positive qualities were and speak well of your previous boss based on it.

By speaking badly about your previous boss, you will be showing the recruiter that you are a resentful person. And he may think that the fault of any altercation was yours. If you had a problem with your previous boss and that's the reason why you are looking for a new job, keep the pride for a moment. Talking badly about him could play against you. Remember, don't complain, don't criticize.

Tell me about your previous job: Once again, don't speak ill about your previous job. However, after having said the positive qualities of that job, you can talk about the shortcomings of that job and why you left it or want to leave it.

Tell me about your work experience: Remember that the important thing is not where you worked, but the achievements you got while you were working there.

Emphasize your achievements and let the recruiter see why it's convenient to hire you.

Tell me about the best and the worst boss you have ever had: Like other questions, the reason of this kind of questions is to know what is the level of respect and loyalty you have towards the company and your superiors.

The best way to answer this question would be with a neutral answer. You can say something like, "I think choosing a single boss as the best would be elitist, since I've learned something from each of the bosses I've had. In the same way, I can't say I had a worse boss. The truth is that I have learned from those experiences. For example, to face challenges, work under pressure, and manage stress better."

Why were you interested this company?: This type of question is the reason why there is a chapter in this book about the importance of researching the company. Many employers use these types of questions to intimidate applicants a bit. But because you have researched about the company before, you can use these types of questions in your favor.

Answer by talking about the work environment of the company, or that you want to work there because you identify yourself with the company's philosophy and values. Anything that has to do with the company and with you. But above all, be honest at all times. The recruiter will be surprised at your easy of speaking when answering these types of questions. And at the same time, you'll be showing yourself as a confident and truly interested person for the job you are looking for.

What are your greatest qualities and abilities?: Explain what your main qualities and abilities are. Afterward, it would not be a bad idea to mention those areas in which you should improve.

If I speak with your previous boss about you, what will be the areas in which he would say you have to improve?: This question refers to those characteristics of your personality that could limit your performance within the company. But having mentioned it when answering about your qualities and abilities, he interviewer will not even have an opportunity to ask this question.

What did you like most and what did you dislike most about your previous job?: Even if the question is, what did you dislike most and what did you like most about your previous job? Make sure to answer first in a positive way, that is, mention first those aspects you liked most about your previous job.

Something must have liked him from his previous job. It may have been your relation with your colleagues, the good working relationship between the staff, the salary, the location, or any other aspect. But to project a better image, you can also mention the challenges you faced in that job.

By saying that the challenges you faced in your previous job were one of the best things about your previous job, your new employer will see in you a person capable of facing the challenges in a globalized world.

Once you have answered what were the most pleasant aspects of your previous job, you can mention the aspects that you disliked most. But never say your previous job lacked any negative aspects. If you say it, the interviewer might ask, "So, why do you want to change the job you have now?" If he asks you that question, I doubt you can answer in an assertive and credible way. Instead, mention some aspects of your previous employment that were not to your liking, with as much diplomacy and discretion as possible. But above all, don't criticize nor complain.

Tell me any anecdote from your previous employment where you have been in a complicated situation. What was your way to solving it?: The interviewer will use these types of questions to know how you deal with problems. If you are a person who lacks patience, it will be difficult for you to fit the personality of many companies.

Try to remember that situation that led you to absolute stress. How did you deal with it? Did things go well? If so, you can tell that anecdote.

The idea is to show yourself as someone capable of facing challenges and difficulties in the best possible way.

What is success for you? / How do evaluate success?: Simple questions but with a wide repertoire of possible answers.

They seem simple, fault-free questions. But actually, your answer to these questions could reveals more about you than you think.

Whatever your answer is, you are actually revealing information about your work ethic, your achievements, your aspirations, your ambitions, and a global idea of your personality.

Think very well what will be your answer to these kinds of questions. Those are very personal questions, and you have to answer them with sincerity. You can answer something like, "For me, success is synonymous with doing things right." Or you can also say something like, "For me, success is achieved when my work gives the best results, or when my superiors recognize the good job I have done."

You can also answer in some way in which you are perceived as someone suitable for teamwork, something like: "For me, success is not about something exclusively personal. I think it's something that can be shared with others. For example, when you work as a team and you get a good job that satisfies everyone."

I remind you that your answer must be personal—something that you really think. That is, based on your own way of thinking. The examples I give you are only for you to get an idea about how can you answer them and what kind of answers employers want to hear.

Once last piece of advice. Avoid being overbearing when answering.

How do you deal with stress and pressure?: This question will help the interviewer to know the level of responsibility you have with your work commitments. Similarly, it's a way to know if you are able or not to work under pressure, something essential in every job in these days.

The best way to answer this question is to state that pressure and stress are really positive things. By doing so, you will be showing yourself as someone capable of facing challenges and maintaining efficiency even in the most demanding moments.

You can say something like: "For me, stress is a positive thing because it stimulates cooperation between individuals. It also helps improve critical thinking, problem solving and creativity."

You can also say: "I tend to prioritize my responsibilities, so I know how to organize my time, even under pressure." Or maybe, something like: "I think the best results come out when you work under pressure. This way, ideas emerge in a more fluid way. I think it's actually something positive and even helpful."

Whatever your answer is, make sure it's an answer that highlights the positivism of stress and pressure. But I have to be clear in this point. If you are really capable of working under pressure, good for you. But if you are not able to work under pressure, you should consider working on it, since nowadays it's something absolutely essential in any job.

What are your goals for the future?: This question is very useful for interviewers. It helps them to determinate your level of commitment to the company.

Are you an ambitious person or are you capable of looking after the company? This is the question that lies behind what are your goals for the future?

Answer in a way that the company can see in you a loyal employee. You can answer something like: " I see myself in a well-established company." You can also say: "I would like to acquire more knowledge, knowledge that is learned only though the practice, that which is not learned at college. I think that knowledge is what makes us more competitive."

Why should we hire you?: There are other applicants out there waiting for the same job. Why should you get the job and not someone else? Think carefully about how you will answer this question.

What qualities do you have?

What can you offer the company that others can't?

The achievements you have obtained in your previous jobs will be very useful to answer these questions.

Your education can also help you answer this question.

When you were studying, there were other students acquiring the same knowledge as you. Why are you better than them?

If you speak any foreign language, say it. If you have extracurricular studies, say it. When answering this kinds of questions, mention anything that makes you stand out from others or that is of interest of the company.

Don't speak badly of the other aspirants under no circumstances. That will not give you any point in favor, but it will subtract many points to you. A person who always criticizes others is a person incapable of working as a team.

How much do you want to earn?: This is perhaps the most intimidating question of all. If you ask for a lot, they probably won't hire you. But if you ask for a little, it's likely that you will get a job with a very low salary. So, how can you answer to this question?

The best is to answer based on flexible intervals. You can answer something like, "I would like to earn between $2,507 and $2,904 a month," for example.

Do a little research about the average salaries around the similar offers as the vacancy that you want to cover. And make an interval according to it. For example, if the average salary is about $3,470, you can say you want to earn between $3,398 and $ 3,530. This way you don't risk getting a very low salary, and at the same time you leave open the possibility of earning a little more.

When you do your research to find the average salary around the vacancy that you want to cover, it's important you do this research according to the location in where you live.

Average salaries differ enormously depending on your place of residence. Salaries in Canada are not the same than salaries in Mexico. And salaries in Germany also different than in Portugal, even though both countries are part of the European Union and share the same currency. Therefore, an engineer will get a higher salary in Germany, where the cost of living is higher than in Portugal.

Each region has an average salary according to the cost of living in that place. Even in the United States, average salaries differ from state to state—even among different cities within the same state. Average salaries in San Francisco, for example, are different than average salaries in San Diego due the cost of living, even when both cities are in California.

Do you have a question?: At the end of the interview, it's common for interviewers to ask candidates if they have any questions. There's only one right way to answer this question—yes.

Make questions. Don't be afraid to ask.

What would be my labor obligations? What challenges can this position offer me? Any point that you have not understood or that has not been explained, don't hesitate to ask. By doing so, you will not only solve your doubts, but you will also show yourself as a person who is truly interested in that job and not just for the financial compensation.

By the way, avoid asking anything related to a salary increase, the benefits you will receive, or the possibility of obtaining a better position in the near future; as well as your holiday periods. These questions express your desire to cover only your financial needs. This way it will be evident that you really don't want to contribute anything to the company.

It's very likely that they will ask you one or more of the questions I have mentioned in the last pages. Try to practice them before the day of your interview. Just make sure you wait a few seconds before answering—one second is enough. Otherwise, it will be evident that you have practiced your answers.

If you were asked any question that doesn't appear in this book, which is very likely, avoid taking too long to answer. As a general rule, if a person takes more than five seconds to answer, it's a clear indication that he is creating his answer. And for many people, this is synonymous with lying.

Practice the questions I have written in this book. Although I recommend you find your own answers, those that fit your personality; always following the instructions that I have given you.

It's important you understand that, whatever the answer you give when they ask you something, it must be an answer that you can demonstrate once you get hired. Otherwise, you could get in risk of being fired.

Abstract questions

The questions above are used to get to know you, as well as your academic and work background. However, these days it's very common for interviewers to ask such abstract questions that may even seem absurd.

These questions have tow objectives: getting you out of your comfort zone—because they know you could practice your answers—and get an idea about your problem solving level.

Currently, companies look for professionals capable of solving problems in the most creative and efficient way. That's the reason for those abstract questions. If you can answer these types of questions with ingenuity and confidence, it's very likely that you will use the same ingenuity in solving problems within the company.

These questions are more frequent in technology companies, such as those large companies of Silicon Valley. They are not usually very frequent in other types of industries. And certainly, they are more frequent in the United States than in any other country. In fact, practically all the recruiters who spoke to me about that kinds of questions, were from the United States. So if you live out of the United States, the chances of being approached with these types of questions are low, although the possibility is not null.

Abstract questions can be as diverse as the companies themselves. I leave you a list with some of the abstract questions that I have knowledge of. Once again, these questions come from my personal experience and the interviews I did. If you research on the web, you could find much more examples.

Finally, don't bother looking for an answer to the following questions because as I already mentioned, the possibilities of being approached with this types of questions are scarce. I just want you to get an idea of the kinds of abstract—and even absurd—questions that some recruiters usually ask.

What are the first three things you do after waking up?

How is your email tray organized?

How is your pantry organized?

How many tennis balls fit on an airplane/boat/car?

What would be your strategy to leave the city in case of a zombie epidemic?

How would you survive if you were sucked into a tornado?

How would you escape a storm if you get caught on a sailboat in the middle of the sea?

If you were an animal, what animal would you be? Why?

If you could have some super-power, which one would you choose? Why?

What car brand and model would you be? Why?

What would you do if you only had one day left?

How would you survive if the plane you're flying in fell?

If you were compared to a board game, which one would you be? Why?

Summary of Most common questions during a job interview

- Review the questions included in this chapter.

- Create your own answers by following the advice I gave you. But adjust them to your personality. The examples described in this chapter are only for references.

- When you get the job, you must be able to demonstrate the answers you gave.

- Don't rush to answer, otherwise it will be evident that you practiced your answers. Doing so will detract from your credibility.

- On the web there are more examples of possible questions during a job interview.

- If they ask you any question that you have not practiced, try to improvise.

- Avoid taking more than five seconds to answer any question. Otherwise, they will think you're lying.

- Consider that some interviewers could ask you abstract questions to confuse you. Try to be clever in answering them. But above all, avoid getting nervous.

Most common mistakes during a job interview

You should already be able to go to a job interview feeling confident about yourself and your capabilities. You already know everything you need to know to increase your chances to get hired. If you have reached this chapter, it means that you have an advantage over the rest of the aspirants—knowledge.

You already know how to make a good resume. You know how important the image is and how to use it in your favor. You know how to adjust your body language and your attitude to look more competent. You have learned how to write a cover letter that will be very attractive to the employer. You have realized how important it's to know the company in which you want to work. You know what kind of clothes to wear to get hired. I have given you several useful tips for your interview. You know what is the best way to behave during your interview. And you've even gone over some of the most common questions recruiters ask during a job interview.

It could be said that you already have all the keys to get the job you want. And we can also say that at this moment you have an advantage over the rest of the applicants. Even so, would not it be better to know what are the most common mistakes during a job interview?

It's possible that after reading through the pages of this book, you would have noticed some of the mistakes you made in the past. Mistakes that you are now aware of and that you can avoid in your next interview.

People say that knowing the history helps avoid repeating the mistakes of the past. The problem is that even if you have made some mistakes in the past, you may not be aware of it. Pride is part of the human being. And it's the same pride what clouds critical thinking; especially when it comes to ourselves. For that reason, I decided to include a chapter to address the most common mistakes of the candidates during a job interview.

Being late for your interview: Punctuality is something very valuable in any job.

Do you want your first impression to be that of someone irresponsible? If you are late for a job interview, it's very difficult to get another chance. Try to arrive at least 20 minutes in advance. But remember, don't advertise yourself until five minutes before your appointment.

Arriving too early to your interview: Actually, it's not as bad as it seems. But arrive too far in advance can be somewhat uncomfortable for the interviewer and his assistants.

The best is to arrive between 15 and 20 minutes before the scheduled time, but not advertise yourself until five minutes before your appointment.

Dressing inappropriately: I dedicated several chapters on this subject, but I include it as a review. Your image is the most important thing for any interviewer, even if they say the opposite.

The image you show may even be more important than your resume. As they see you, they treat you. Or in this case, as they see you, they hire you.

Being impolite: The interviewer is not the only person you should please. When you enter the company's building, you will be approached by several people with different functions within the company. The mere act of arguing with the cleaning staff, for example, may be a good reason to not hire you.

Excessive use of lotions and perfumes: Many people abuse lotions and perfumes. A habit that is annoying to other people. And it's probably that the interviewer dislike the excessive use of perfumes and lotions too. The best is to use lotions and perfumes sparingly. Consider lotions and perfumes as accessories, not as personal grooming items.

Wearing sunglasses: Sunglasses have become a fashion accessory, although it is also true that many health professionals, especially ophthalmologists, recommend them whenever they have a UV filter.

They are really useful accessories to care of our eyes from the harmful UV rays from the sun. Unfortunately, many people don't realize that they can also *block* communication between two people. The mistake is not wearing sunglasses, but to keep them during the interview.

Some people continue the interview wearing their sunglasses indoors. Other people choose to place their lenses on the upper part of their foreheads—another serious image mistake.

You can wear sunglasses on your way to the interview, but store them once you get to the place where the interview will take place. Don't hang them in your clothes, much less on your head. Keep them out of the sight of the interviewer.

Not introducing yourself: One of the biggest mistakes when entering an interview is forgetting to introduce yourself.

When you enter to your interview, greet the interviewer with a firm handshake, keeping eye contact.

If the interviewer is a woman and you are a man, don't shake her hand unless she does it first. If she doesn't extend her hand to you, just say hello and introduce yourself.

Regardless of the sex of the interviewer and yours, don't greet the interviewer with a kiss—unless he or she does it first—let alone with a hug.

Forgetting the vacancy that you are applying for: I know it seems ridiculous. But believe it or not, there are aspirants who forget the vacancy they are applying for.

Either because they have sought different vacancies in different companies, or because nerves played them a bad turn, forgetting the job you want will make you seem disinterested for it.

Talking too much: There are people who tend to talk too much. They are people who offer too many details, even when they were not asked. Very typical of people desiring attention. And it's a very annoying behavior for most people. And it's also possible that the interviewer is within that majority.

This doesn't mean that you must respond with closed answers; those that stop the flow of conversation and create awkward silences, that is, answers that only include the words *yes* or *no*.

You must prepare a thirty-seconds speech. And when you answer the interviewer's questions, avoid giving more details than necessary.

I'll show you an example.

If the interviewer asks something like:

"Where did you study, and what did you decide to study?"

And you would answer:

"I studied Administration and Top Management at UCLA. **It was a wonderful experience. Can you believe that it's very easy to make friends there? Or course, the academic programs are very complete, although teachers are somewhat strict. Perhaps that's the reason why it has been considered one of the best universities in the United States.**"

Pay attention in the bold section. Do you think that information was necessary? Do you think the recruiter is interested in that kind of information?

If after reading this example you consider yourself as a person who *talks too much*, I recommend you learn to reduce your words.

Next time you talk with someone, be aware of the situation. Try to analyze your behavior when speaking. Do you talk too much? If so, try to practice when talking to people.

Not talking enough: This mistake may seem contradictory to the previous one. But I will explain it in more detail. At the end, you will realize that it's not contradictory at all.

In the previous point I explained the importance of not talking too much. That is, not saying what is not interesting at that time.

WELCOME ABOARD: MORE THAN 200 TIPS TO MAKE THEM HIRE YOU 195

This point, on the other hand, talks about the importance of speaking enough. There is a big difference between enough and too much.

It's possible that an authority figure, such as the interviewer, may be intimidating to you. Don't worry, you are not the only one. But that intimidation that a figure of authority can generate in you, can make you somewhat shy and withdrawn at that moment, regardless of your true personality. Especially when we know that our future job is at stake.

Obviously, we don't know the interviewer. And we don't want to look like disrespectful nor overfamiliar people either; because, as I mentioned in other chapters, the image and the attitude you project are very important during a job interview. And so that we are not perceived as disrespectful and overfamiliar people, it's normal that we avoid talking about more because of the simple fear of saying something inopportune.

The problem is that this fear can become so strong that many people will answer with closed answers, those answers that block the flow of the conversation and creates awkward silences. That is, monosyllabic responses that usually are *yes* or *no*.

In a chapter, as well as in the previous point, I mentioned the importance of making a thirty-seconds speech. It's a very effective way to break any barrier of communication and trust between you and the interviewer. If you are able to make a good thirty-seconds speech, I guess you will not have any communication problems.

In order to reinforce what I have explained, I will leave you an example so that you understand it better.

Imagine that the interviewer asks you:

"What did you do in your previous job?"

And you answer:

"I was the general manager."

In this case, the interviewer really wanted you to describe the responsibilities you had in that job. He wanted you to be a little more specific.

A better answer would have been:

"I was the general manager of the branch. I was in charge of employees performance and customer service. I promoted internal campaigns of personnel motivation. I also developed some advertising strategies at the regional level, with which I managed to considerably increase the profits in that branch."

Unlike the previous mistake, all the information presented by the applicant in this example was relevant to the question asked by the recruiter. The answer lacks any impertinent hesitation. That is what *talking enough* means. It means enriching your responses with the most pertinent details, but without reaching hesitation.

Using your mobile phone or any other mobile device: There is nothing more annoying than being ignored. And it's something that the interviewer will not tolerate.

Don't answer your phone or make any call during the interview. Don't answer any text message either. In fact, before entering your interview, your should turn off any mobile device. Yes, turn them off. Don't put them in vibrator or airplane mode. If you are using a Bluetooth device, turn it off and keep it out of the interviewer's sight.

Wearing a Bluetooth device in your ear will not make you seem more important, but it will make you look more arrogant and disinterested about the job.

Interrupting the interview to answer a call, or answering a text message, is a clear indicator that you are not a person capable of ordering your priorities—a good reason to not hire you.

If your phone rings during the interview, the interviewer will not care in the least if you forgot to turn it off. That will immediately ruin your image before the interviewer.

Enter the interview with food and/or drinks: In one chapter, I talked about the importance of having a good breakfast before going to the interview.

Many aspirants make the mistake of skipping breakfast and decide to buy some sandwich or a bread roll, or take some fruit with them; besides buying a drink, usually coffee.

The problem comes when you have to enter the interview and decide to enter with food or drinks. When you do that, you are projecting an image that communicates inefficiency in the administration of your time. And at the same time, you will also project an a very bad impression by *impregnating* those aromas along the office environment.

The same applies to any candy, especially chewing gums. Chewing gums are often used by people who obsessively worry about their breath, or by people who suffer from anxiety.

Chewing a gum will help you dissolve anxiety and stress, but it's not a good idea to enter the interview with the gum still in your mouth. If you think that chewing gum will help you control your anxiety while waiting for your interview, don't forget to get rid of it before entering the interview.

Not preparing yourself to answer the questions: One of the biggest mistakes of many aspirants is to pretend that they will be able to improvise each of the questions the interviewer asks. When an aspirant doesn't anticipate the questions that they will ask him, the risk of being seized by the nerves increases considerably. That makes you take more time to respond and with that, you are also in risk of contradicting yourself in the following questions.

Using supports to answer the questions: Many people uses supports—notes—when they have to expose some topic. It's a habit they carry from their years as students. A habit that is not well seen during a job interview, nor in any professional environment.

If you are unable to answer the questions they are asking you, don't use any notes or help cards.

Maybe this seems an absurd advice. But trust me, there are people who have tried to use some kind of support to answer the questions during a job interview. And the results are always negative.

Not taking care of your body language and your attitude: Many aspirants believe that by choosing good clothes and dressing appropriately they will be immediately hired. The problem is that they don't pay attention to their body language and attitude.

Remember that the image you project is more that just choosing the right clothes. You can dress with luxury items that favor your body shape and skin tone. But even so, if your attitude is not adequate, your image will be negative. Make sure you take care of your posture and your attitude. Make sure that your posture and body language state the message your really want to communicate.

I dedicated a whole chapter on this topic. If you have forgotten, I recommend you reviewing it.

Going to the interview with a bad appearance: Make sure you don't go to the interview when you are sick, much less when you have a hangover. Or even worse, being tired or sleepy.

Interviewing someone who is sick can be annoying and unpleasant for the vast majority of interviewers; especially when shaking hands. On the other hand, if you go to the interview tired, or even worse, with a hangover, you will be immediately perceived as someone unreliable to work in that company.

Generally, appointments are assigned by human resources personnel. And many times they will not ask you what day do you prefer to go. And if sick that day, it may not be all lost.

If you wake up with a flu the day of your interview, choose to wear a shirt or blouse in blue, preferably in sky blue. We tend to associate the blue color with cleanliness. For this reason, companies that sell detergents and other cleaning products tend to make them that color. In addition to making you look more *clean*, blue color make you look more sincere and reliable. It's undoubtedly the best option you can take if unfortunately you wake up sick the day of your interview and could not change the date of your appointment.

Carrying other people with you: An unusual mistake, but equally a mistake. Avoid taking other people with you to your interview, especially if they are children. Unless you are going to a group interview, your interview will be personal.

Forgetting basic information: Make sure you can remember the basic information about your education and your work experience, as well as the vacancy you are applying for.

Make sure to remember the name of your previous bosses, the names of the companies in which you worked and, above all, the position you want to get in that company. It seems incredible, but some aspirants forget which is the position they want to cover just at the moment when the interviewer asks them.

Not knowing enough about the company: This is perhaps the most common mistake among applicants. Going to a job interview—to a company where you want to work for—and not knowing anything about that company.

I have spoken several times about the importance of knowing the company in which you want to work. Being informed about the company will not only improve your confidence during your interview, but it will also allow you to adjust your resume to the profile the company is looking for, which will increase your chances of getting an appointment for an interview and most likely the job.

Not carrying copies of your resume and reference lists with you: Many applicants assume that the interviewer has read their resume. In fact, the staff of human resources are those who schedule the appointments with the employer. And it's possible that the person who interviews you has not read your resume in detail.

Be sure to take several copies of your resume with you, with the best possible presentation, as well as some copies of your reference lists. Some copies may be requested at the end of your interview.

Speaking badly about other candidates: Avoid speaking badly about other candidates. Talking badly about other candidates will not increase your chances of being hired. In fact, you will only let the interviewer know that you are a person who doesn't know the meaning of the word *ethics*.

Speaking badly of your previous bosses: The interviewer is not your therapist, so don't try to vent on him your frustrations about your previous boss. In fact, by speaking badly about your previous boss, the interviewer will only be able to see that you are a disloyal and a troublesome person.

Speaking badly about the company you previously worked in: Once again, don't try to vent in the interviewer your frustrations about the work you had in the last company where you worked in. This way you will only be showing yourself as a disloyal person.

Showing yourself indifferent to any aspect of the company: Avoid showing yourself indifferent or against any aspect of the company. Don't criticize the logo of the company, its philosophy, its values, its work environment and so on.

Showing yourself indifferent to any aspect of the company indicate you are a person who lacks of flexibility to adapt different situations. If you have any suggestions for the company, it's best to wait until you have been hired.

Complaining: Whether it's about your previous boss, your co-workers, the previous company you worked in, the city's transportation system, your current work situation, whatever it is. Don't complain. Nobody likes a complaining person. And much less to your interviewer.

Avoiding eye contact with the interviewer: By avoiding eye contact you are only showing yourself as a submissive person; or even worse, the interviewer could see you as a liar.

Lack of eye contact doesn't mean someone is lying. In fact, that's just a myth. But unfortunately, most people accept that myth as a fact. And many people cling to believe that a person who doesn't make eye contact is a liar. It's best to avoid any risk and make eye contact with the interviewer.

Make sure you are keeping eye contact with the interviewer throughout the interview, but make sure you don't look threatening. Review the previous chapters for more information.

Nervous tics and bad behaviors: Playing your hair, biting your nails, whistling, drumming your fingers, and any other behavior that may be perceived as bad behaviors should be avoided.

Not smiling: Many people don't smile during the interview. On the other hand, some even tend to smile more than they should.

In most cultures, smiling means being in the best position to negotiate. By smiling, we establish an emotional bond of empathy, which will be very beneficial for the aspirants. It's advisable to smile when we greet anyone in the company or when we meet with the interviewer.

The smile is an excellent resource to make a good first impression, but you should not abuse this resource. If you smile too much, you may seem nervous or worse, you could look like a psychopath.

Showing yourself desperate for the job: Some applicants make the mistake of telling the interviewer that they need the job, or even worse, that they need the money to pay off their debts.

If you are desperate to get the job, it will be evident to the interviewer that you are only interested in your financial situation and that you are not interested in the company at all.

Avoid showing yourself desperate for the job. But above all, avoid mentioning that you need employment and money.

I wrote about this topic in other chapters, in case you don't remember it, I recommend you go back and review them.

Abusing the sense of humor: While it's true that humor can generate empathy and goodwill in others, it's also true that it's not a good to abuse a sense of humor. And much less during a job interview.

Avoid laughing at inappropriate times. And above all, don't make unnecessary jokes. Remember that you are in a job interview, not in a meeting with your friends. And more important, they are evaluating you.

Interrupting the interviewer when he is speaking: Some people are very impatient when it comes to answering questions. They answer questions even when the person who is asking them has not finished speaking. A very serious mistake.

Never interrupt the interviewer when he is speaking. The interviewer is paying attention when you are talking, and you should do the same.

Don't interrupt him when he is speaking. He will not forgive you.

Not paying attention to the interviewer when he speaks: Incredibly, some applicants tend to ramble during their job interviews. Some of them don't even pay attention to the questions the interviewer ask them.

An employer in Manhattan told me that he has interviewed several applicants who always asked him to repeat the question he just asked few seconds ago.

"How is it possible they make me repeat a question that I asked a couple of seconds ago?"

I honestly could not believe it when he told me that. But it's true. Some applicants don't pay enough attention to the questions during their interviews.

Pay close attention to the interviewer's words. Otherwise, he will realize you are a person who lacks concentration. In that case, you can be sure they will not give you any chance within the company.

Not having questions: It's very common that at the end of the interview, the employer asks you if you have any questions. And it's also very common for applicants to answer saying they have no doubt.

A human resources specialist in Atlanta told me, "If an applicant wishes to work in a company, he will have some doubts about the vacancy he is applying for, the work environment, his responsibilities in that new job, or about the company. If you are not really interested in that vacancy, that is, if you are only interested in that job to get out of your financial problems, then you will have no doubts. You will only look for a job for money, without caring about anything else."

Even if you were not asked if you have any questions at the end of your interview, It's advisable to ask questions about those points that have not been clear. It's about asking questions about the job, the work environment, the obligations and responsibilities you will have within the company, and any other relevant topic.

Avoid asking questions related to a possible salary increase, vacation periods, work benefits, and any other question that can reveal any selfish desire before the company.

Not thanking at the end of the interview: Many people leave the interviewer's office without thanking the interviewer for his time. When an applicant doesn't appreciate the time that the interviewer invested in him, that person will be considered as unfriendly, rude, and with superiority complex; undesirable aspects in any worker for any company.

When the interview is over, stand up and thank the interviewer for his time. Say goodbye to the interviewer with a firm handshake and a smile.

Leaving the office in a hurry and with a downcast posture: When the interview is over, many aspirants leave the office in a hurry. And in the worse case, with a downcast posture.

Even when the interview is over, they keep evaluating you. Show yourself as a confident person while leaving the office and even the building. Keep an upright posture and walk towards the exit without any haste. This way you will be showing yourself as a person who shows confidence in what he does—a worthy person for the job you are applying for.

Summary of Most common mistakes during a job interview

IMPORTANT

Unlike the summaries of any other chapter in this book, this summary doesn't contain a list of tips. Don't take this list as a series of tips, but as a list of the most common mistakes during a job interview. Mistakes whose explanations you will find in this chapter.

Be sure to read in detail the explanation of each of the mistakes mentioned in this chapter. If you skip this chapter, you could be in risk of misinterpreting the mistakes mentioned in this list.

- Arriving late for the interview.
- Arriving very early to the interview.
- Dressing inappropriately.
- Being impolite.
- Excessive use of perfumes and lotions.
- Wearing sunglasses during your interview.
- Not introducing yourself.
- Forgetting the vacancy that you are applying for.
- Talking too much.
- Not talking enough.
- Using your mobile phone or any other mobile device.
- Entering the interview with food and/or drinks.
- Not preparing yourself to answer the questions.
- Using supports to answer the questions.

- Not taking care of your body language and your attitude.
- Going to the interview with a bad appearance.
- Carrying other people with you to the interview.
- Forgetting basic information.
- Not knowing enough about the company.
- Not carrying copies of your resume and reference lists with you.
- Speaking badly about other candidates.
- Speaking badly of your previous bosses.
- Speaking badly about the company you previously worked in.
- Showing yourself indifferent to any aspect of the company.
- Complaining.
- Avoiding eye contact with the interviewer.
- Nervous tics and bad behaviors.
- Not smiling.
- Showing yourself desperate for the job.
- Abusing the sense of humor.
- Interrupting the interviewer when he is speaking.
- Not paying attention to the interviewer when he speaks.
- Not having questions.
- Not thanking at the end of the interview.
- Leaving the office in a hurry and with a downcast posture.

Comments and incredible stories from recruiters

When I interviewed the recruiter professionals, whose advice were very useful to write this book, I got some comments that were funny and caused me some skepticism. In some cases, I could not believe what they told me. After all, some of those stories were so absurd that I certainly could not believe them.

I decided to included some of those comments and anecdotes in this book. I believe they could be useful to you, or at leas they will help you avoid falling in the same mistakes.

Image and attitude

"I don't care what your personality is. If your image is not the best for this company, don't think you will get a job with us. And I'm pretty sure that all employers think the same way I do."

—Marco Ferrari, manager. New York, the United States

"I was waiting for the applicant for about half an hour. When he arrived, he apologized for being late. I could not believe what I was looking at. He was dressing black pants and a white long-sleeved shirt. The shirt was so wet with his sweat that it seemed transparent. Being honest, I had to put up with the urge to laugh. How could he have thought that he would make a good impression that way? I granted him the interview, although it was only an act of courtesy. Actually, I never though to hire him after seeing him soaked in sweat."

—Alicia Gutierrez, human resources manager. Guadalajara, Mexico

"One day I received a young man in my office. He was well dressed, but with a very strong body odor. I told him I could not interview him until he took a shower. Unfortunately, there is no polite way to tell someone that his body odor is very strong. He never came back."
—Sofía Villarreal, assistant manager. Barcelona, Spain

"Just yesterday, a young man came here for his job interview. He arrived dressing a football t-shirt and he had not combed his hair. I refused to interview him."
—Gerardo Urbini, manager. Buenos Aires, Argentina

"There are aspirants who arrive *bathed* in perfume. Can't they take a shower? When someone with too much perfume arrives, I just want the interview get over in order to take a breathe. Possibly I will not even pay attention to his speech."
—Gerald Blanc, human resources. Brussels, Belgium

"One day, a young man came to his interview. He was wearing a black suit, a white shirt, a red tie and... white sneakers! My assistant, who was inside the office with us, could not help laughing. And although I tried to be discreet about, her laughter was contagious. The young man showed a gesture of shame and retired after a few seconds."
—Michael Johnson, human resources manager. New York, the United States

"I think the worst impression was given me by a young girl in dark clothes and gothic appearance. She had several holes in her face. She had three perforations in her right ear, one in her nose, one in her lower lip, and one more in one eyebrow. She had pink highlights on her black hair. And her eyes had the same gothic style. Honestly, it scared me a little."

—Rachel O'Brian, human resources. Los Angeles, the United States

"Many people don't know it, but social skills are one of the things that all employers look for. Most companies will prefer someone with good social skills rather than a person with good credentials but lacking in social skills. Customers feel more comfortable with those people who demonstrate having social skills. And those types of employees are more productive in the sales area."

—Eric Anderson, manager. Sydney, Australia

"Employees are the face of the company, since they are the ones who deal directly with customers. Therefore, the image and attitude they have before the customers is the most important thing for me."

—Kevin Mark, manager. Chicago, the United States

Interviews

"I've seen a lot of things since I've been a manager. But I think the most absurd thing I've seen in this office was an applicant who came to her interview with her boyfriend. When I asked her boyfriend to leave the office and she told me that she had brought him to help her with any question she wasn't able to understand, that is, he was her translator.

I asked her if she was serious. The vacancy specified that we needed someone competent in English language."
—Germán Hernandez, manager. Santiago, Chile

"I remember an applicant who asked me to hurry because her best friend was waiting for her at the mall to go to breakfast. I told her not to waste my time."
—Álvaro Montez, human resources. Monterrey, Mexico

"It bothers me when someone asks me questions about this company. Don't they know the internet? If they are looking for a job in this company, it's supposed to be because they've researched about it."
—Joan Walden, human resources manager. Mountain View, the United States

"Turn off your mobile phone before entering my office. Seriously, turn it off! Nothing bothers me more than the ringing of a telephone during an interview. It's totally rude."
—Greg Schulz, manager. New York, the United States

"If someone comes and he will talk badly about his previous boss or about the company where he was working, or if he will come to complain about his problems, better not to waste my time. Instead of looking of a job, I would recommend him finding a therapist."
—Peter Arlington, human resources. Liverpool, United Kingdom

"I asked a question to an applicant, and he gave me a strange answer: 'I don't know. Could you move on to the next question?' I was perplexed by his attitude."
—Mariana Alcántara, human resources. Medellín, Colombia

"All the people who come into my office believe they are the best at what they do. Actually, I have several options to choose from. And nobody is good at anything until they demonstrate their productivity within this company."
—Alex Smith, manager. Houston, the United States

"I think I got the worst impression when one of the applicants came into my office with a dish of tacos. He was eating while he was waiting for his turn. The smell of fried food permeated the entire office. I asked him to retire. It was the most disgusting thing anyone has done in this office. Although now that I remember it, it makes me laugh."
—Félix Montenegro, manager. Mexico City

"A couple of years ago, one of the applicants asked me to hurry up with the interview because he wanted to watch the World Cup matches. Obviously, it was something rude to me."
—Rubén Martolini, human resources. Montevideo, Uruguay

Resume

"On one occasion I received a six-page resume. It made me lazy to read it. Applicants should know that if their resumes are too long, they will

go straight to the trash. We have many documents to review. And many of them are of higher priority."
—José Gutierrez, human resources. Mexico City

"A few years ago, I received a resume where the applicant detailed all his academic information. Literally, all his academic information! From kindergarten to college. He had also included all his previous jobs, including his small jobs as a child. I had so much fun reading it that I read the entire ten pages. But as a tip, I think a resume should not go over two pages."
—Marie Leblanc, human resources. Quebec, Canada

"Actually, I only read the resume if the cover letter seems interesting to me."
—Erica Paige, human resources. Seattle, the United States

"If you are going to send you resume by email, don't mark it with urgent priority. You will only make us see you as a nuisance."
—Marco Panetta, human resources manager. Zurich, Switzerland

"Applicants should know that we are going to judge them based on their email address. If you use an allusive or ironic name in your email, rest assured that you won't be hired. Imagine that one of my clients receives a business card from one of my employees with a ridiculous email address like sexyman@mail.com. It's totally ridiculous. Don't they know that their name is their personal brand?"
—Joe Stephen, sales department manager. Boston, the United States

"The more languages the applicant speaks, the more I convince myself to hire him."
—Angelica Rossi, human resources. Geneva, Switzerland

"If someone includes his social media profiles in his resumes, rest assured that we'll review them to better understand his true personality."
—Anne Carlton, human resources. London, United Kingdom

"A week ago, I received an excellent resume. I was impressed with the applicant's credentials and his work experience. But there was a problem. He forgot to include his contact information."
—Richard Liang, manager. Singapore

"The worst resume I received was one that was printed on colored sheets. It had been written with a font with rare and illegible letters. I didn't even read it. I'm looking for professional people, not immature people."
—Carla Asunción, manager. Panama City

Behavior

"Don't argue with anyone. Everything is recorded by the security cameras. And bosses don't want troublemakers inside the company."
—Gabriela Díaz, manager assistant. Miami, the United States

WELCOME ABOARD: MORE THAN 200 TIPS TO MAKE THEM HIRE YOU

"I don't trust anyone who play with their hands. It desperate me."
—Carlos León, human resources. Madrid, Spain

"Be an adult. Otherwise, we'll discard your resume immediately."
—Josefina Martí, human resources. Buenos Aires, Argentina

"I don't like applicants to pat me on the shoulder or on my back. We are not friends. I don't even know them. They should be more respectful."
—Mario Palmer, manager. San Jose, Costa Rica

"You can dress elegantly. But if your behavior is not congruent to your dress, then you don't deceive anyone."
—Antony Carman, consultant. Los Angeles, the United States

"Once a young man arrived greeting everyone as if they had been lifelong friends. Obviously, he was trying to be social. But it was obvious that he lacked social skills. All the people he greeted, including me, showed some suspicion at his strange behavior."
—Marc Stephan, human resources. Paris, France

"It's one thing to be social and another, very different, is to be annoying."
—Gisselle Kurtz, manager. Frankfurt, Germany

"I don't understand why aspirants try to deceive us. We have listened to several others before them. We already know all the possible deceptions."

—Ashton Clever, consultant. Calgary, Canada

Conclusion and final advice

After reading this book, you may have noticed a number of mistakes you made in the past. Mistakes that may have cost you the chance to get a job.

Now that you have read this book, you have enough tools to find a job and get hired. Now you know how to manipulate the odds in your favor. You have a superior advantage over other applicants, who are ignorant of the knowledge you have acquired by reading this book.

My greatest wish for you, is that you can find a job that really fascinates you; a job that you can go with impetus and not with a feeling of obligation. Although being honest, I think what motivates you the most when applying for a job is the salary you will receive. And I can't blame you—nobody can. After all, we need money to survive. And a sure way to get money on a constant basis is through employment.

I know that finding a job today has become a very difficult task. But I trust that, with the help of the advice I've given you in this book, you can get that job you're looking for.

If you manage to find a job where you feel comfortable, a job that you truly love, or at least, a job that takes you out of your financial problems or that only helps you improve your economic situation; if this book at least helped you find a job, I would believe I will have successfully fulfilled my mission—to help people improve their work situation.

I hope that after reading this book, you have regained the confidence to face another job interview. I hope that from today, you begin to forget all the setbacks you had in the past. I would like you to begin to regain your confidence in yourself.

I sincerely hope that you achieve all your work objectives. That's what inspired me to write this book in the first place. And nothing would make me happier than knowing that I could help a person by writing this book, and that thanks to me, at least one person has one less concern in his life.

But I also have to be totally honest with you.

You may not be the only person to read this book. In fact, if someone recommended this book to you, it means that at least one other person has read it and therefore, it would be very naive of you to think that you will be the only person who could benefit from reading this book.

What I want to say is that other people will also have the same tools that you have obtained by reading this book. And if you are lucky enough to read this book a few weeks after it release, you can be sure that you will keep a superior advantage over the other applicants.

But if you have read this book long after its release, it's very likely that other people besides you are using the same knowledge that you have acquired.

So, if many people besides you have read this book, does that mean that you can no longer have an advantage over other applicants? The answer, dear reader, is a lucky no.

Even if other people have read this book before you, you can still have an additional advantage over them.

I will give you some final tips that will be of great help to keep an advantage over other applicants. And unlike most of the advice I've given you until now, these final tips depend solely on you. And that's the reason why it doesn't matter how many people read these tips, because each person will take them individually according to their lifestyle. And so, each person who takes these tips will forge their own advantage personally.

All the tips I'll give you below are so you can improve your reputation before any employer. And in case of a crisis and its consequent reduction of personnel, you can survive it.

Bring yourself up to date

The first advice I can give you is to be updated. If you are an administrator, bring yourself up to date with the new administrative systems. If you are a lawyer or an accountant, bring yourself up to date with the latest legal and fiscal reforms in your country of residence. If you are a graphic designer, bring yourself up to date with the new technologies in design. If you are a fashion designer, bring yourself up to date with the new trends. No matter what you career is, bring yourself up to date as much as you can. The simple fact that you have finished attending school, doesn't mean you have to stop studying and accumulating knowledge.

Many people believe that when they leave college they stop being students. And it is precisely these people who stay behind in life. Because by not accumulating more knowledge than they acquired in the college, these people begin to become mediocre people compared with those who are bringing themselves up to date and accumulate more knowledge over time.

I'm not suggesting you go back to college, but you can try to learn new things to bring yourself up to date. Remember that when you were a student there were many other people studying in the same classrooms, and every year there are more graduates out there. This increases the demand for jobs, but vacancies almost never increase. And if you stop learning, there will be people more prepared than you looking for the same vacancies you want to cover. And they will be the most valuable people—those with more knowledge—those who take the available vacancies.

You may try to excuse yourself by saying you don't have time. But I will ask you a question. How much time do you lose by watching TV or surfing the web without doing something productive? Be aware of it. And consider for a moment that all that time you waste in front of your TV or your computer, you could either invest it in reading a book or taking a tutorial that allows you to further increase your knowledge.

To bring yourself up to date and increase your knowledge, you can read books during your free time. You can also take an online tutorial or enroll in a diploma course. You don't even need to leave your house. Today there are too many online courses you can take from home. Nowadays, whoever doesn't learn something new, is because he doesn't want to. You may also consider attending workshops and conferences. Those a great ways to bring yourself up to date and get more knowledge.

Remember that everything you learn can increase the value of your resume. And don't forget that you were not the only person who attended college.

There are thousands of new graduates every year, but job offers tend not to increase, which increases unemployment and competition for existing jobs. And constant learning will give you a greater competitive advantage over all those who stop learning after leaving college.

Currently, being updated with the new technologies is one of the skills that companies value most.

There's a reason why many companies begin to emphasize the priority for young talent. And it's about the management of new technologies. Even if you are young, remember that technological world is advancing more and more by leaps and bounds; so it would be a good idea not to underestimate you need to bring yourself up to date with new technologies.

Learn new things

My next advice is very similar to the previous one—learn new things.

Learning means discovering new possibilities. The more knowledge you acquire, the more productive and valued you become.

Unfortunately, when people take a bachelor degree program, they only focus on it and are indifferent to other areas. If you studied medicine, it would be possible that you only read about new medications; as well as new instruments and surgical technologies and everything related to your career. But why not learn about administration? Or maybe you can learn something about accounting or public relations.

Can you imagine how valuable you would be for the hospital if apart from your obligations as a doctor, you could be useful in the administrative department, or as a hospital spokesperson? They may even place you in another department, with a better salary.

I'm not talking about going back to college and taking another bachelor degree program. I'm talking about enriching your general knowledge during your free time. I speak of reading about those subjects that, although they don't belong to your career, can be very useful in the company in which you work for. Certification courses are also very useful because they will not only allow you to acquire new knowledge, but it's also possible to obtain a diploma that supports that you have taken those courses.

When there are layoffs, the first to leave are those that are less useful to the company, those that are expendable and easily replaceable. But when you show that you are more useful than your colleagues, human resources department will think it twice before considering your dismissal.

Learn languages

My next advice is still about learning new things. In fact, this is no longer an option. Currently, it's an indispensable requirement in many jobs.

Learn a language and if possible, learn more than one.

Nowadays, globalization is more important than in previous years. And companies really value those employees who can speak several languages.

If you are reading this book and you can understand its content, it means you speak English.

English language is definitively the most important language in the world. If a group of people from different countries enter a room, how will the communicate each other? By speaking English, of course.

English has become the most important language around the world, and you may believe that you have a great advantage because of that. But unfortunately, it's the opposite.

English-speakers are well-known to be indifferent when it comes to learning other languages. In fact, the non-English speaking world see English-speakers as the worse language learners.

English-speakers are so comfortable by speaking English that they usually don't bother to think about learning other languages. After all, why should they learn another language if they already speak the most important language in the world?

If you are a native English-speaker and you don't speak another language, it's easy to think that way. But let me ask you some questions. How many people are living in the United States right now? How many people are living in Canada? How many people are living in the United Kingdom, Australia and New Zealand? And how many people speak English as a foreign language around the world?

English is the third most spoken language in the world, counting only native speakers. And it's the second most spoken language if we take in account those who learn English as a foreign language.

As there are millions of English-speakers around the world, and many of them speak also other languages, don't you think they are leaving you behind in this globalized world?

If you are a citizen of the United States, for example, and you only speak English, why employers will prefer you over another person who speaks English too but also speak Spanish? Don't you believe that a bilingual person would be considered as a better option than you?

Remember that the more value you can offer to the company in which you want to work in, the more chances are to get the job. And if you already have a job, in case of a massive cutoff, if you offer more value than others, you will be safe.

Speaking English is an advantage to those who don't speak it as mother tongue, but if you speak English and no other language, then you are not special to any company. After all, they can find a lot of people like you in just few minutes.

When it comes to getting advantage over others, speaking other languages than English becomes in a very attractive advantage for you. Some of them will be more helpful than others to you, depending on where you live. And this is because in addition to English, there are other languages that are very important in today's world. Languages that will undoubtedly give you a greater competitive advantage wherever you go. In fact, as I already mentioned, speaking only English is no longer synonymous with competitive advantage. And even being bilingual is not synonymous with competitive advantage anymore in some companies, as nowadays the competitive advantage is for people who speak more than two languages.

Spanish is a very important language nowadays. Especially if you are living in the United States, where Hispanic community is growing by leaps and bounds.

Spanish is frequently required in many industries within the United States because there are a lot of people—who are potential customers for any company—who only speak Spanish.

Spanish is especially required in hospitals, schools, legal offices, government offices, sales departments, management positions, hotels, restaurants, touristic attractions... Basically, if you are living in the United States, nowadays it's almost impossible not listening Spanish every day.

Spanish is the second most spoken language around the world, second only to Mandarin Chinese. It's spoken practically in the whole

Americas. From the south of the United States to Argentina, practically all the continent speak Spanish, being Canada and Brazil the only big countries in the continent in where Spanish is not officially spoken. Even so, Spanish is frequently spoken both in Canada and Brazil. This makes Spanish language the only language around the world that can open the doors of a whole continent to you.

Also, Mexico is one of the biggest markets for American and Canadian companies. This makes Spanish language one of the best options for many residents in the United States and Canada.

In Europe, on the other hand, Spanish is not as important as in The Americas, but it's an interesting language for Europeans, as Spanish economy is getting better. In any case, some Latin-American countries are getting relevance in the global economy. And if one of your goals is to venture in the global market, remember that Spanish can open you many doors in a whole continent.

French has been considered for many years as the second most important auxiliary language, after English. And although today French language has lost that status in favor of other languages, such as German in Europe, Spanish in The Americas, and Mandarin Chinese in Asia, it remains one of the most important languages in the European Union.

Undoubtedly, a very useful language for those professionals who are involved in international trade within Europe; as well as for fashion designers, chefs, engineers, and tourism professionals.

German is nowadays the second most important language in Europe after English. As Germany has become the most powerful economy in Europe in the recent years, German language has become a very important language for work.

German is also the language with the most native speakers in Europe; being official in Germany, Belgium, Liechtenstein, Austria, and Switzerland. A very favorable language for those interested in international trade with Europe; as well as for businessmen, engineers, and economists. Companies value employees who speak German fluently due to the complexity of the language. The good news is that it's kinda easy to learn for English-speakers, as both languages come from the same linguistic family.

Mandarin Chinese has gained great notoriety due to the Asian giant's economic expansion. And while it's true that most Chinese are learning English to cover the most important business positions, Western companies begin to appreciate when one of their employees shows some fluency in mandarin Chinese. And as it's considered a very difficult language to learn, companies appreciate employees who manage to at least have conversations in that language.

However, specialists warn on learning Chinese. Because Chinese is a tonal language and you must learn about 50,000 characters to barely read a newspaper, experts and some managers think that you may be too old to master Mandarin Chinese. Many of them even recommend learning other languages, maybe two, instead of just trying to learn one language you won't master as an adult. In this case, native speakers are those who could take this advantage.

Russian is another language that begins to have certain presence in the global market. And it's very useful for those who work for an international company.

While it's true that it's a very complex language, Russian is very useful these days and will remain so for many years to come.

Russia is part of the BRICS, a group made up of five countries considered as emerging economic powers. For this reason, Russian language is very popular today. Not to mention that Russian is the *lingua franca* in Eastern Europe, especially in countries that were members of the former Soviet Union; being spoken in Russia, Belarus, Kazakhstan, Kyrgyzstan, Latvia, Moldova, and Ukraine. Undoubtedly, a very useful language for those wishing to venture into international, tourist, and oil companies. Currently, it's one of the most requested languages in Europe.

Like Russia, Brazil belongs to the BRICS group. For this reason, Portuguese language is considered today as a very important language in the global market. A very useful language for those who want to venture into international companies due to the rise of Brazil as an emerging economy.

Portuguese language is pretty close to Spanish. This means that if you learn Spanish, you could learn Portuguese in a very short time.

Arabic is another language that can increase the value of your resume. It's the common language of the countries of the Middle East, countries with the largest oil resources in the world and consequently, with an excellent purchasing power. A very important language for those interested in civil engineering, due to the high rates of recruitment of foreign engineers in the Middle East for the modernization of their cities, as well as for those interested in the oil industry.

Another language with some relevance in the modern world is Japanese. Despite being spoken only in Japan, the fact that the country of the rising sun is the third global economy, and one of the most important trading partners of Western countries, makes Japanese an attractive language for employers. And unlike what is usually thought, most Japanese can't speak English.

Japanese citizens, on the other hand, are some of the most important customers for tourism companies around the world—mainly in Europe—which makes Japanese an ideal language for those professionals who work in tourist companies.

Korean is another language that is taking some relevance in the global market due to the large presence of Korean brands, mainly electronics, around the world.

Korean language is very useful in industries focused on import and export due to the strong global presence of electronics brands based in South Korea. Undoubtedly, a very useful language for professionals involved in the logistic industry.

Make yourself noticed and be more productive

Another tip I can give you so that you can keep your job even when there are layoffs is to stay visible and important to the company.

Companies value those employees who are more visible and therefore more important. In fact, when there are layoffs, they begin by those who are invisible and unimportant—those who are easily replaceable.

You can also try to be more productive. Try to create strategies that help the company grow, but above all, be sure to take credit for those strategies. In other words, try to generate achievements within the company.

Try to get noticed in your work, especially before the eyes of your superiors. But you must also be careful not to appear puffed-up when you get significant achievements.

Being more productive gives you an additional advantage. In case of a dismissal, or if you are looking for a better job, you will have increased the value of your resume with those achievements you have obtained by being more productive.

Flexibility

Try to be more flexible. Try not to get categorized into a specific role within the company. Avoid being too rigid with your work schedule.

Companies prefer those employees who are not afraid to change their routine or place of residence in favor of the company. Flexibility may seem to sell your soul to the company. But you must remember that if you manage to obtain certain recognition within the company in which you are working, that recognition will help you to have a more attractive resume, what will help you find a better job in the future if you wish.

There are many inflexible employees out there and they are easily replaceable. Flexible employees, on the other hand, are very scarce and highly valued.

Specialization

Specialization is another of the things that increase the value of your resume and therefore, your permanence in any company. Get enrolled in courses, certifications, and specializations that are focused on the areas in which you work. All those courses will increase the value of your resume and will help you reduce the possibility of being fired when a massive cut of personnel is made.

I think I have no more advice to give you. I suppose that the advice I have given you, not only in this chapter, but throughout the pages of this book, will be of great help to find a job, maintain it and perhaps get a better position in a short time.

I don't know where you are living, but the advice I have given you will serve you anywhere around the world. The most important thing is that you understand them and put them into practice. Having read this book will not help you if you don't put into practice the advice I mentioned.

The world is not going to change. That's something we should all accept. But there are always two options: complain and lament for the world in which we live, or try to understand the situation and face the life we have. I prefer the second option. At least, I avoid self-inflicted suffering while try to find a solution to a problem that I know will persist for a while longer.

What I mean by this is that the world is going through times of crisis. And we can't wait for that to change in the future. It could improve, yes. But it could also get worse. Will you sit there waiting for new jobs to open, or do you prefer to face the crisis and find a job even when the odds seem pessimistic?

The advice I have given you will help you adjust the odds in your favor. But for there to be a real change in your life, you must make the decision to act.

In the African savanna, if the gazelle doesn't run, the lion eats it. But if the gazelle runs, the lion will not eat that day. The same happens in our concrete jungle. If you don't get the job, another person will get it. If you get it, another person will lose it. And although it seems a cruel vision of life, in a way, it is.

And nothing will change with just to want it. You have to take action if you really want to do something—if you really want a change.

Getting a job will be the first step towards a better life. A life in which your economic problems are a thing of the past, or at least, are minor. A path to financial independence that, in a way, is something that most people in this world seek.

This book is just the first step to a better work life. And as your working life progresses, you will realize that in reality, most of these tips will not only help you get a job, but also will be of great help to increase your credibility and confidence in any field of your life. And certainly, all that is better than just getting a job.

Acknowledgements

I must confess I never thought about writing this book. Everything had started as a simple project for college. But not of this would have been possible had it not been for a group of people who, despite being busy all day, decided to give me a few minutes of their time.

I have nothing left but to thank them for everything—their time, their patience, and all the advice they gave me at that time.

My gratitude is not in vain. Not only did they help me get good jobs when I managed to get out of college, but also, without even knowing it, they helped many more people.

Many of them also had to make an effort to brake the language barrier, especially those who don't speak neither English nor Spanish as their main language. Not understanding perfectly the languages that I speak, they could have simply said they were too busy and didn't have time to give me an interview. But instead, they made a great effort to understand and make themselves understood.

I don't believe there are words in any language that can express the gratitude and admiration I feel for all of them.

I would like to especially thank Philip Müller, Joe Stephen, Gisselle Kurtz, Joan Walden, Greg Schulz, Ashton Clever, Angelica Rossi, Alicia Gutierrez, Sofía Villarreal, Marco Ferrari, Gerardo Urbini, Gerald Blanc, Michael Johnson, Rachel O'Brian, Eric Anderson, Gabriela Díaz, Enrique Salvatore, Carlos León, Rubén Martolini, Kevin Marc, Germán Hernandez, Alvaro Montez, Peter Arlington, Mariana Alcántara, Alex Smith, Félix Montenegro, Erica Paige, Marco Panneta, Paula Castilla, Anne Carlton, Richard Liang, Carla Asunción, José Gutierrez, Marie Leblanc, Jason McCormick, Josefina Martí, Mario Palmer, Antony Cartman, Marc Stephan, Roberto Paletta, and Antonella Navarro.

And although I am aware of being the author of this book, it's likely that I would not have had enough material to write a whole book if it had not been for all the help I received. That's why I think I should share the credit with all of them. For without their help, this book might not exist.

All the advice I received has been very useful for me during many years. And I hope that now they can also be useful for many more people.

About the Author

MATIAS ASTORI. Passionate and studious of behavior and human relations. He began studying neurolinguistic programming in 2005. Later he began to study other related disciplines such as psychology, cultural anthropology and neuroscience principles, among others.

In 2014 he decided to publish a book to help people get a job successfully. This book was originally written and published in the Spanish-speaking world, due to the strong labor crisis in Spain and Latin America during those years.

After the success of his first book, and seeing that many of the sales were in the United States, and because many English speakers began to request an English version, Matias Astori decided to create a version for the English-speaking world, being he himself who worked on that version, due to his linguistic abilities in both English and Spanish.

He currently works as a full-time author and spends most of his time working on new installments, as well as personal investigations.

www.ingramcontent.com/pod-product-compliance
Lightning Source LLC
Chambersburg PA
CBHW031617210526
45464CB00004B/1613